Rational Thinking, Government Policies, Science, and Living

Rational Thinking and Government

by Dr. Sanford Aranoff

Rational thinking starts with stating the problem or goal, using the correct relevant principles, applying logic to arrive at conclusions, and finally checking for empirical verification or falsification.

This book gives many examples of people thinking and acting in ways that are not rational. The primary purpose of the book is to educate, so that our society will be better off.

Please discuss these ideas with each other and help make the world a better place for all of us. Thank you very much in advance for your efforts!

Table of Contents

1. Introduction

It is vital for both individual and national survival to think rationally and critically. Although we all agree to this statement, unfortunately we do not understand what rational thinking is. We do not know how to think rationally. Most of our lives involve interactions with other people, such as friends, colleagues, family, and co-workers. Our emphasis is on getting along successfully with others, for we cannot live by ourselves. Rational thinking takes second place after the importance of successful give and take with other people. This is how we are. Very few of us are truly self-reliant and clear thinkers.

Rational thinking starts from basic principles, uses logic, and looks for empirical verification or falsification. We also need critical thinking to examine the accepted principles.

Our schools stress behavior, not critical thinking. The corporate and military environments incorrectly stress following the leaders, instead of stressing focusing on the problems and the goals, striving to do what is best.

Most Americans, especially well to do people, are expert salesmen. (BTW, "men" is short for "human", and so one can correctly speak about a woman salesman. I do not have to say "saleshuman" or "salesperson".) A salesman is a person who clearly explains the virtues of the product, and is very enthusiastic about it, while downplaying the drawbacks or competitors' products. When people buy the product the salesman is hawking, the salesman makes money.

Lawyers are salesmen. They downplay the opponents' ideas. Politicians are salesmen. Pundits and journalists, on television and in print, are often salesmen, as they get their funding by corporate or government donations.

What is strange is that many university professors are salesmen. They are swept up with the hype, and fail to think clearly and rationally. May I remind my fellow scientists that many major scientific developments began by individuals or small groups with ideas very different from the majority prevailing opinions.

Due to our lack of critical thinking, we have been making the terrible mistake of accepting the falsehoods of progressive thinking. The profound stupidity of our leaders and public is amazing. This stubborn wrong thinking is also present in scientific work. This stupidity includes not only politics and physics, but also religion and normal sexual living.

This book is a collection of articles I wrote on these various topics.

We simply cannot rely on our wise leaders, our politicians, our university professors (including Nobel laureates), and political pundits and journalists. Our excessive reliance on these people is as foolish as the reliance of the ancient Greeks on the Oracle at Delphi. We human beings must think carefully ourselves, check and examine our thoughts, and discuss our ideas with others. The ideas and thoughts in this book may help you in this very important task.

Be strong and courageous. Do not give up. Good luck!

-Dr. Sanford Aranoff

1.1   Welcome topic

Essays by SA – Sanford Aranoff

After receiving my PhD in theoretical physics from New York University, I taught physics at universities for several years. I moved into defense work, primarily software engineering, for financial reasons, to support my growing family. Several years ago, I returned to academia. The long break made me carefully examine the guiding principles of rational thinking. In graduate school, I discovered a major principle, which I word to myself as, "What is the problem?" This means one has to focus on the goals. What bothered me was why I had to wait until graduate school. The answer is that most people do not think this way. My parents and teachers did not think this way. The American defense industry has many failings because defense workers focus on the boss' requirements. The extreme case was one company that issued daily Statements of Work (SOW). Each day the government official in charge had to tell the research scientists and engineers what to do. The result was following orders, not thinking rationally focused on the goals. American soldiers follow orders, while Israeli soldiers keep their focus on the goals. For this reason, Israelis are superior fighters.

This book is a collection of items that I wrote to various people in leadership positions. People were doing things wrong, to be blunt. People fail to understand what has to be done.

I spent a great deal of thought in these articles. Please give these ideas serious consideration.

1.2   Purpose of the book

The American society is in very serious trouble. The powerful, wonderful economic engine is stopping. Leaders who oppose use of fossil fuels are thwarting the blessing to our nation that fossil fuels have given us. These stupid actions are bringing curses to our country, and destroying the blessings. Our leaders and commentators spend a lot of time explaining their ideas. However, since the explanations are intrinsically false and illogical, the vast amount of words and time do not help our nation to be more prosperous, safer, and healthier. The reason for the false explanations is the lack of proper logic. Not only politicians, but also our scientists are guilty of being illogical. This book is an effort to clarify this with the hope that people will think properly and act better to solve the problems facing them. When we discuss political and scientific leaders, we of course cannot omit religious leaders who also mislead with faulty logic. When a business or bank sells below cost plus expenses, it will go bust. Yet the government often compels businesses to sell below cost, and is then surprised at the results.

Individuals need to understand themselves and their personal needs. Failure to understand themselves and others results in unhappiness and misery. Sex is a subject that is sadly misunderstood. This book discusses the nature and compelling needs of sex. The hope is that people will think deeply and carefully about these ideas, and discuss them with each other, with the result of leading happier, healthier, and more prosperous lives.

Enjoy and good luck!

2. Politics

Al-Kaeda is an idea. How do you fight an idea? Islam is an idea. How do we fight the idea that Muslims must kill all those who oppose a one world government under Muslim law? How do we change people? There is only one way, proven over the millennia of human existence, to change people. **This is by education**. We must use our military to *force* the people of Afghanistan not to teach murder and suicide. We are totally ignoring education. This is what our soldiers must do. Arrest the teachers of murder and hold them in jail until the end of hostilities.

Chavez. Talking to people who voted for Chavez,

asking how were they so stupid. Reply – he promised many good things. The previous parties were always fighting, etc. It is imperative that Americans learn and educate others about Venezuelan politics for the uncanny similarity to the rise of Obama. We ignore events in other countries at our peril. Another example is the almost complete lack of coverage of the field hospitals Israel is operating in Haiti, hundreds of patients daily.

America is the greatest free country!

Let us all lift our heads up proudly and state America is the greatest country in the world, like none other! Only in America do we believe in individual freedom, rule of law, property rights, self-reliance with minimum government help, and the belief that making financial profit is the best way to help and advance society.

No other country has this attitude. Let us adopt the attitude that we can help the world by educating other countries (and our fellow Americans) to the very great importance of this attitude. Let us call on our leaders and educators to proclaim the call for freedom!

Look at other countries. Our friends the Saudis do not give women the freedom to drive their own cars. We need to send Sec. Clinton to Saudi Arabia to educate them on American ideals of freedom, instead of Obama bowing to the Saudis.

Our allies the European countries limit the freedom of people to start businesses by extremely excessive government regulations, resulting in rampant high unemployment. We need to educate Germany and others to allow people to have more freedom starting businesses, instead of our silent attitude to their unhealthy socialism.

Our trading partner and source of most of our manufactured products, China, believes in government control of the economy, and points to its recent successes as proof of the success of socialism. Buy China if we must and cannot buy America. However, we must lecture them at every occasion the importance of freedom, even if this makes them angry. The American motto is "Give me freedom or give me death!" We are going to talk to everyone about freedom, and refuse to be silenced, even if we lose business or lose our jobs.

The Pope said people should live honestly and not strive for profits. When we meet the Pope, instead of bowing and accepting this, we should stand tall and speak proudly for the importance of profits for the wonderful future of the human race. America believes that salvation comes from freedom and striving for profits. Let us not fear the Pope, and reiterate this at every occasion. Let freedom ring!

Americans must return to living as free people, and not bowing down fearful of others. When leading American executives go to Congress and are asked how they got there, they must stand up proudly and say we are a free people and can travel by private jet if we choose, and Congress has no right to hint that we did anything wrong, saying we should drive. When a former Governor says that Obama was nominated for President because he is black, and then is accused as being a racist, she must say that she has the right to speak freely. It is not racism to say he was nominated because he is black. A mayor must say that he will choose the very best people as firefighters, in order to best save lives and property, and will ignore any possible lawsuits restricting his freedom demanding blacks with lower test scores be firefighters. When a judge rules that the city must have blacks with lower scores, we must stand up and say this judge is not fit to judge Americans, and we must fight for justice and freedom and not let her become a Supreme Court justice.

When we travel abroad, as individuals or as national leaders, we will praise America and exhort the local people to follow America's example of individual freedom and minimal government. We will speak in loud clear voices, using all the means at our control, such as radio, television, advertising, and the Internet, to get our message of freedom, regardless of whether they want to hear what we say or not. We will not tolerate any objections from Arabs who do not want women to have freedom or from Chinese who do not want anyone to have freedom. We will not give technology to China that will permit the government to restrict Internet sites. We will march in the streets of Rome in front of the Pope proclaiming freedom and the rights and benefits of working for profits. Instead of going to Rome and acting like the Romans, we will proudly speak about our ideals of liberty, and work to educate others.

As a free people, we are always aware of rational scientific thinking. We will not accept any government action forcing one to accept Catholic or Islam thinking. We will not accept any statement from the President such as "The science is settled," for scientists always have the freedom the challenge current thinking. Truth in science is not determined by a majority vote but by logic based upon basic principles and examination of situations in other areas and times. We will maintain our rational thinking, and not be persuaded by those who say the world is coming to an end unless we impose steep taxes on people.

We will encourage young people to enter politics in order to use their creative intelligence to solve problems, corruption and hatred in our society and in the world. We will not mock politicians with whom we disagree saying he is stupid, or she is a quitter, unless there are actual verified acts of misbehavior.

We will solve our health problems, no thanks Mr. Obama for your efforts to solve our problems with our money. Just let us alone and let us have our freedom. No taxes on medical insurance, whether or not from an employer. Enough with the government mandates on insurance and different rules in different states.

We must demand the freedom to drill everywhere for oil and gas. We need to have the freedom to use coal and nuclear energy without government interference with taxes and unnecessary regulations. We need the freedom to have windmills on the oceanfront, without the shore residents stopping it. We will do it ourselves, and become energy independent. We do not want you, Mr. Obama, telling us what to do. Just do your job executing the laws of our country, and stop trying to control us and take away our freedom!

Anarchy. My country, America, is entering a state of anarchy. People do what they want, ignoring rules, laws, and, yes, even the Constitution. People do this with impunity. This is widespread, and very dangerous to our security and prosperity. Let us focus our attention to the frequent lapses of law, and fight for what is right and for the rule of law. Let us fight for the greatness of the American ideals, and shout down those who say America is a bad country, having committed evil. We are not perfect. This is good, not bad, for perfection is impossible. We Americans must be proud of our goals and our way of life, and fight political leaders and interest groups that oppose and object to the American way of life.

Here are some examples. Two years ago the Big

Three auto manufacturers testified in Congress. A
Congressman asked them how they got there.
They said they flew. This was not the way to
respond in an official Congressional hearing. The
correct proper response was saying Congress had
no need to know how they got there, as Congress
must not interfere with private business.
Individual freedom from the government must be
kept sacred. It is not valid to say that since they
were asking for money they had to politely
respond to all questions. They were not begging
money from a wealthy source, but instead asking
Americans to help the company for the
self-interest of Americans. Any other reason is
wrong. The punishment for giving information to
the government that they should not have given
was that the next day they drove down, rather than
fly with their personal planes. Unfortunately, no
one criticized Congress for asking this
unacceptable question, not realizing that
Congress' action in asking this question was an
example of anarchy.

President Obama pressured BP to put up $20
billion into a fund to compensate victims of the
oil spill. Congressman Joe Barton said this was a
"shakedown". Eugene Robinson wrote that
Republicans think "it's more important to kneel at
the altar of radical conservative ideology than to
feel any sense of compassion for one's fellow
Americans." According to Robinson, the
President did a good thing out of compassion.
This goes along with Obama's ideal judge who
has "compassion". This is contrary to the ideal

judge in the Hebrew Bible who judges fairly, as it states, "You shall not pervert justice by having empathy for the poor or glorifying great people; instead, you shall judge your countrymen with justice." This principle is embodied in the American legal system. A judge who has compassion for the poor is a judge who perverts justice. The President who asked for money from BP prior to a proper legal hearing and ruling by a judge is a President who perverts justice, a President who creates anarchy.

The nomination of Elena Kagan for Supreme Court Justice is a sign of anarchy, for she expresses that anarchist principle of compassion.

The President issued an order stopping drilling in the Gulf. A judge ruled the moratorium is not valid. The Administration responded saying "We will appeal." This is anarchy. You do not just appeal because you disagree with a judge's decision and have the money to appeal. You appeal because you feel errors were made during the trial. Since the government gave no reasons for the appeal, the statement "We will appeal" is anarchy and destructive.

People who disagree with Obama's action in getting the money from BP are criticized saying they are taking BP's side, and since BP is a bad company, having caused such damage, they should not take BP's side. This statement is not an American statement, but a statement by an anarchist. There is no BP side until the issue is discussed in court, where each side can present facts and issues as they see them. Prior to the court hearing, there are no sides.

The passage of the health care law is anarchy. It mandates that insurance companies have no lifetime coverage limits. Mathematically, no limit means infinite (I teach this mathematics in my university). Infinite coverage is mathematically impossible. Since the law has an impossible clause, the law is not valid. There should be no need to wait for a Supreme Court ruling. Anarchy and destruction result from impossible laws. Another example of an impossible law is the law requiring banks to give mortgages to poor people at the same rate as people with good jobs. This is the *Community Reinvestment Act.* Since it is impossible for banks to operate this way, they went bankrupt. What is scary is that the CRA is still on the books. The government still asks banks to do the impossible. This is clear anarchy.

Any law that Congress passes and the President signs that clearly violates the Constitution or mathematical logic is anarchy and very dangerous to our country. It is a mistake to think we need to wait for a ruling from the Court on the constitutionality of legislation. Congressmen and the President have taken oaths to uphold the Constitution. Any action that they do that violates the Constitution is a violation of their oath, is immoral, and grounds for impeachment. Our leaders must use their common sense determining what is Constitutional and mathematically reasonable. The American people must be active in demanding removal from office Congressmen or the President who espouse and encourage anarchy. It is up to us to defend our country!

The Articles of Confederation
High school students learn about the *Articles of Confederation* and the *Constitution*. After the American Revolution, our country was run for a decade under the Articles of Confederation. As a substitute teacher, I ask students about this. I ask what was wrong with the Articles, and why did they decide to write the Constitution. Students do not have a good answer. We must give our students an explanation. Then I say that the UN is run in a fashion very similar to the Articles. The question is why we cannot learn from history. We know that the Articles did not work. Why cannot the UN be organized like the Constitution, with a world federal government collecting taxes, as the present arrangement does not work? Each country would be a state in the UN federation. Just as we do not need passports to go from New York to New Jersey, we should not need passports to go from Mexico to the U.S. Just as New York and New Jersey cannot fight a war with each other, the U.S. and Iran should not be able to fight a war with each other.

Indeed, many people are working towards this goal. For example, President Bush refused to use the military to prevent Mexicans from migrating to the U.S., as Bush and President Fox planned to integrate Mexico with the U.S. President Clinton issued an Executive Order saying employers cannot require English only in the workplace, as Clinton was working towards a UN federation with all languages equal.

President Obama is working towards a national health plan so that all Americans will have medical insurance. This is the first step towards a UN federation, where all people in the world will have medical insurance. Are we not concerned about the health of all peoples?

There are many powerful interests working towards this goal. These people are idealistic, and feel deeply that we cannot have the present situation of separate independent countries. It is necessary to have a central world government in order to bring security and prosperity to all the world's peoples. This philosophy is reflected in the *Security and Prosperity* bill, an agreement between Mexico, the U.S., and Canada.

The powerful wealthy people who are working towards this universal goal are aware of the overwhelming strong opposition. President Bush always denied plans to unify Mexico and Canada with the U.S., but actions clearly shown that he was lying. The goal is to weaken the American economy so that the government can then say they are acting to revive and save the economy, while secretly laying the groundwork for the goal of universal government. Obama's talk and actions are clear. Senseless and stupid on their face, but clear for the goal of secretly working towards a world government.

Devoutly religious Moslems also work towards a universal government. Their goal, however, is not a government modeled after the U.S. federal system, but based upon Sharia law. The Moslem goal conflicted with Bush's goal, and so Bush had to fight the Moslems in Iraq and Afghanistan.

Obama is a puppet to the powerful, secret universalists. They set him up, financed his election, and instruct him on policy. There is no other logical explanation. Obama is clearly a stupid person if we look carefully on what he actually says. For example, Obama said that the Boston policeman Crowley acted stupidly, while saying that he did not know all the facts. No intelligent person would criticize a policeman the way Obama did while admittedly not knowing the facts. Obama's support of the ousted president of Honduras, ignoring the Supreme Court's ruling that he is ineligible, is a further sign. Obama's statement that natural growth of Israeli "settlements" is unacceptable is a sign of Obama's stupidity, for no rational person can make such a statement. Notice that Obama does not spend time alone analyzing the complex issues for which his is responsible. The reason is that he knows he is not responsible, but simply acting a role and following orders. *Obama is not in charge of America.* We need to find out who really are running our country.

We need to break the secrecy and bring out to the

open the issue of a universal federation. If Obama is secretly planning this, Congress should hold impeachment hearings.

Personally, I am opposed to a universal federation. Are you? I am opposed to Clinton's Executive Order regarding English. I am opposed to us not using our military to defend our borders. I oppose racism saying Jews cannot live in certain places, for the sake of peace in the Middle East.

Who is our President Obama? Of course, he was born in HI, as there are newspaper reports of this birth. We all know that newspaper reports cannot be changed. Or can they?

Obama's confident poise is phony, for no human being can be confident about national policy questions. The facts and issues are more than a single human mind can properly deal with. When a medical doctor expresses full confidence in a procedure, we should not trust the doctor but go elsewhere. All procedures have statistical probabilities of success. Ignoring the statistics is intellectual dishonesty. We know not to trust confident salespeople. We know not to believe confident television commercials. Obama's confidence clearly indicates his dishonesty.

Let us listen to quiet reflective reasoning. Let us discuss the idea of a UN federation. Let us discuss whether capitalism and individuality is better than central government planning. Let us discuss this, giving reasons and examine supportive and contradictory evidence. The fact is that America was founded as a nation independent of others in a free-market capitalistic system, and has been successful for centuries, does not mean it should continue. Maybe central planning, Communist style, is better. Let us discuss this openly. However, let us not move towards Marxism without talking whether we want to adopt Marxism.

Personally, I vote for the successful model of individualism as practiced in America until FDR changed things. Reagan changed them back, against FDR, and all Americans, and indeed the entire world, benefited. What do we want now - FDR or Reagan?

China
We live in dangerous times, and, sadly, we cannot rely upon our governments to adequately protect us. Bridges collapse because of faulty design. Inadequate government inspections cause us to lose lives, health, and property.

It is very hard for the average citizen to fight corruption that leads to faulty and dangerous structures. However, there are some things we can do.

China sells us food containing poison and toys painted with lead. We must choose not to buy any product made in China. We have to be resolute and determined to search for non-Chinese products, and decide to do without if we cannot find what we need.

Fresh fruits and vegetables are different. In the interests of our health, we should try as much as possible not to buy imported food. If the only apples we see are from Chile, we can buy other fruits. There is no reason why food has to be shipped across oceans, polluting the air, when we can get excellent food right here. The same is true for wine. California wine is fine, and we do not need European wines.

Let us help each other out by helping Americans. This will help our pocketbooks and our health.

Americans must understand that prosperity, health, and national security follow from our ideals of freedom. Let us fight as hard as we can against all those who want to trick and compel us to give up our freedoms. Let us fight Obama and the Democrats in order to avoid another world war. Let us fight their emotions and illogic. Let us challenge them who is paying them to say the wrong dangerous things they say. Let us insist that less regulation and taxes will make us all healthier, wealthier, and wiser.

If we in America are to succeed as a nation, we need to study our past great culture, Western Civilization, know our history, and understand various economic philosophies. We can teach this in our schools and have adult education programs. Political leaders should be required to take a few courses in Western Civilization before they can run for high office, just as doctors need to take courses in anatomy. Let us not forget the noble and successful values of our founding fathers, encoded in the U.S. Constitution. These ideas of individual freedom, choice, minimum government, justice, and property rights proved so successful as to make America the great country we are.

The American founding fathers were not the first to develop the ideal of a sound economy based upon individual freedom and limited government. The ancient Israelites, ancestors to today's Jews, were the first.

America began by the revolution against Great Britain. Judaism began by the revolution against ancient Egypt. Egypt, the world's superpower, was a society that believed in strong central government that controlled most aspects of people's lives. America celebrates the Revolution on July 4. Judaism celebrates the revolution by the holiday of Passover, "the time of our freedom." Passover stresses choice and asking questions, not mindless acceptance of authority. The goal of the Egyptian was a good place in Heaven. The goal of accepting Judaism and acting in accordance with the religion is a good society in Israel. Christianity and Islam also keep the focus on Heaven, not building society. For example, a Jew would never permanently lose his means of production, his property, for it will always be returned in the Jubilee year. Safety nets are intrinsic to Judaism.

These Jewish ideals practiced in the Middle Ages, permitted Jews to successfully engage in commerce in spite of the severe centuries-long economic depression in Europe.

Sadly, people do not understand the Jewish idea of freedom and choice. People who like to control others find Jewish ideas an obstacle. This is why despots hate Jews.

Unfortunately, we Americans have forgotten the noble ideals of our founding fathers and the Jewish people. For example, FDR nearly destroyed our economy by his strong government policies. Here are some books proving this: "*New Deal or Raw Deal?*" by Burton W. Folsom; "*The Forgotten Man*", by Amity Shales; and "*FDR's Folly*" by Jim Powell. Obama is also acting to destroy America by making the government strong.

FDR did not let Jews escape the Holocaust, but let them die rather than live and come to America. He knew that Jews are a free-spirited questioning people who would interfere with his big government plans. When Obama said that Israelis should not expand "settlements" even for natural growth, one wonders what should Israelis do, abort the children, like Pharaoh, the ruler of ancient Egypt said? Obama is like FDR, a big government person.

If we study history, we will understand that our

prosperity and happiness comes with small government. We need to focus on historical successes, such as the founding of our great country, the United States of America.

Just returned from a visit to Israel. Went swimming in Sachne, a natural heated large lovely pool near Beth Shan, south of Lake Kinneret. They have an area where preschool children can swim. My daughter went with a long dark dress and long sleeves, in spite of the summer heat. She complained that she has to dress that way, as she does not want to expose herself to men.

The next day I went alone. While preparing myself, an Arab family came in. I said to the man, "How are you?" He replied, "Thank God." I then started talking to the woman. I told her that my Jewish daughter was dressed just as she was. She replied that there is no difference between Jews and Moslems; however, Christians are different, as they dress immodestly.

The young Arab mother was wrong. Islam is similar to Christianity but not to Judaism. Islam and Christianity are selfish religions, for the goal of both religions is to the "a good seat in Heaven" (to quote my Dad). Judaism's goal is building the society in Israel. Whenever one reads the Hebrew Bible about the rewards for obeying God, it is benefits to the society and the country Israel, not the personal good to the soul as in other religions. Let us clarify this by looking at the beginnings of

Judaism, which began in ancient Egypt.

Egypt was the world's superpower. It was a statist society, with government control over everything. It was successful for many centuries. The Bible tells us that Joseph, the acting ruler of Egypt, moved people around the country. That is, the government told people where they could live.

A society ruled by strong government controls depresses economic advances and is very unpleasant to people. The Israelites left Egypt after negotiations, sanctions, and finally military action killing many Egyptians. Talking and sanctions failed. War was the only way to achieve freedom. This was very similar to the American Revolution in every respect, where talking and sanctions did not work, with only war, killing many British people, was the only way to achieve freedom.

The Egyptian society was based upon the belief of a good life after death. The Hebrew Bible never mentions the Hereafter. This point is discussed extensively in the Talmud, the book of Jewish laws and traditions. The reward for good deeds is a better society.

During the Middle Ages rabbinic authorities formalized the legal structure of Judaism, with Rambam (Maimonides) listing the 613 commandments that God gave to Moses. The first commandment is to believe in God. Ramban (Nachmonides) disagreed. The idea is that one cannot command belief, for in Judaism if one verbally states belief in God but actually does not believe in God, the verbal statement is nothing. Ramban replaces belief with the commandment to live and settle in Israel.

The controversy between Rambam and Ramban exists today. Many feel the primary aspect of religion is belief in God. Ramban feels the primary aspect of Judaism in settling in Israel and building the society and the country. Ramban's idea of Judaism is foreign to most Western thinkers, who focus on religion's goals for a better world. American Jews do not get it, erroneously thinking Judaism means going to synagogue, whereas Judaism means living in Israel, raising a family, and have the children raise children in Israel. The Bible tells us that when David contemplated leaving Israel he said how could he leave and worship other gods. David said that leaving Israel is contrary to Judaism.

Israel must be a Jewish state, and not a state like other states. Israel cannot be part of a New World Order, a universal federation, nor can Israel be part of a universal Sharia society. This is the source of the friction.

Israel needs the land it conquered in the defensive war of 1967 for places where American Jews can move to live. When America insists Israel withdraw for peace, Israel must say peace will come with America's help, specifically, the migration of American Jews to the West Bank for the sake of the Jewish ideals expressed in the Torah and for peace. Israel needs America, but not American money or diplomacy, but American Jews to live, visit, or vacation in Israel. American Jews can work as teachers in Arab schools and universities. The reply to the demand for withdrawal must be a demand for American Jews. Peace will be achieved by joint Israeli-Arab ventures in tourism.

Note that Jewish acceptance of some Torah ideals does not conflict with a person's atheistic beliefs. Modern Israel was founded in the 1930's by Jews who were committed atheists. The proportion of atheists among Israeli Jews is far greater than the proportion of atheists among American citizens. Nevertheless, the founding Zionists accepted the history of the Jewish people as expressed in the Hebrew Bible, the Torah. Although they do not observe the rituals, they do observe many of the moral teachings.

Judaism has a moral message to the world, with the goal of changing the world's people. The only proven way to change people is by education. Hence education is one of the primary values of Judaism. For this to work, educators must be developed in the Jewish state, Israel. Peace will come by education, pioneered by Israel.

America catastrophically ignores education in the war on terror. America permits schools to educate future terrorists. We fail to apply the lesson of World War II, where we forced Nazi education to stop. Israel must freeze all peace talks until more Americans come to the West Bank and Gaza to teach Arabs modern Western values.

American Jews forget the Jewish value of building up the Jewish society in Israel. Instead, American Jews are infused with Christian values that they mistakenly take for Jewish values. For example, the Christian value of rewarding oneself (life in Heaven) is a value that Jews like Madoff and Goldman Sachs have absorbed, so that they focus on their rewards (while alive), ignoring harm to others. The correct Jewish approach to life is to build up the society for the living.

I spoke to a man, age 31, married with a few children, a neighbor of one of my daughters in Israel. He spends this time studying Torah, supported by private donors. The study of the Torah, that is, the Hebrew Bible and literature, is considered one of the most important commandments, for which the reward is huge. This young man said he studies Torah in order to help the state of Israel. He did not say he spends his time studying Torah because of the huge reward. Of course, you and I may disagree, saying studying Torah does not help the country. This is not the point. The point is his stated goal. The goal of Judaism is to help Israel, not to have a better afterlife. This is the unique message of Judaism, which sharply contrasts with Christianity and Islam.

The failure of people to understand the lack of a

selfish goal in Judaism is responsible for most of the animosity towards Judaism. People cannot understand why Jews are doing what they are doing. The problem is that Jews also do not understand it either. Zero Mostel said it is because of "Tradition". Zero was wrong. Jews act in order to build a good society for Jews in Israel. Even during the many centuries when Jews lived in places like Russia, they prayed and longed thrice daily for a return to Israel. Israel is the core of Judaism. The reward for being a good Jew is seeing your children and grandchildren growing up in Israel. This is what brings happiness to the Jew. Think about these things, and try to understand them. Exercise your free choice to do the right things.

Corporations

We have to think about the unfair treatment we receive from corporations.

Slavery is the legal fiction that a person is property. Corporate personhood is the legal fiction that property is a person. Like abolishing slavery, the work of eradicating corporate personhood takes us to the deepest questions of what it means to be human. And if we are to live in a democracy, what does it mean to be sovereign? The hardest part of eliminating corporate personhood is believing that We the People have the sovereign right to do this. It comes down to us being clear about who's in charge. We need to modify the Constitution to state explicitly that corporations are not persons.

Honduras

The Supreme Court of Honduras ruled that Zelaya is not eligible to be President. The U.S. President, Obama, declared that Honduras must take Zelaya back as President.

Suppose the U.S. Supreme Court ruled that President Obama was not born in HI but in Kenya, and so is not the President. What will happen? We know. Obama will ignore the ruling of the Court. Since the Court knows this, knowing how Obama demanded the Honduras court be overruled, our Court will not take the case of Obama's birth.

We American citizens must strongly protest Obama's terrible actions demanding Honduras' court be overruled. We must never forget Obama's actions, as they clearly demonstrate the type of person Obama is.

General McChrystal

The Israeli soldier is different from the U.S. soldier. The Israeli is focused on the goals, doing what is necessary, and, of course, obeying the superior officer. The American is primarily focused on obedience. President Obama said in his message to schoolchildren the needed to pay attention. I wrote to the President disagreeing, saying their goal is understanding and asking questions. We all must be focused on what is the problem. This is what I wrote in my book *Teaching and Helping Students Think and Do*

Better. President Obama accepted the resignation of the commanding officer in Afghanistan, Gen. Stanley McChrystal, because he publicly disagreed with the President. Commentators all agree that McChrystal was wrong in disagreeing. I disagree with all the commentators. If we cannot permit people to publicly disagree, we are not permitting them to think rationally. If we cannot permit our soldiers to think rationally, we will not win the wars we fight. We must learn from the Israeli military how to think and fight.

In contrast to Americans, Jews raise their children to ask questions. On Passover, the Jewish Freedom Holiday, children ask the *Four Questions*. People do not like others who question a lot, and this is why people do not like Jews. However, we must understand that questioning and expressing doubt is an essential activity of rational human beings, including soldiers.

Iraq

The Democratic Party's victory in the November 7, 2006 Congressional elections convinced Iran and Syria that they are on the verge of a great victory against the US in Iraq. Iranian and Syrian jubilation is well founded in light of the Democratic leadership's near unanimous calls for the US to withdraw its forces in Iraq.

Baker made clear that he will recommend that the administration negotiate a withdrawal of US forces from Iraq with Iran and Syria. That is, he is putting together a strategy not for victory, but for defeat.

Baker fervently believes that U.S. foreign policy should revolve around being bad to its friends and good to its enemies.

Baker as the man who accepted the 1989 *Taif Accord* that ended the Syrian-sponsored Lebanese civil war by sacrificing Lebanese sovereignty to Assadian fascist occupation in the name of regional stability.

Baker is remembered as the man who abandoned Iraq's Shi'ites to their fate at the hands of Saddam after the US failed to assist them in their post-Gulf War rebellion which the US itself had encouraged. Finally, no doubt they noticed that Baker's law firm Baker-Botts is representing the Saudi government in the 9/11 victims' lawsuit against the kingdom.

Another similarity between Israel's retreat from Gaza and northern Samaria last year, its withdrawal from south Lebanon in 2000, and the proposed US retreat from Iraq today are the obvious consequences of such a retreat for the US, the region and the world. Far from bringing peace and stability, as the champions of the withdrawal policy mindlessly claim, a retreat will cause more war, more instability and more suffering in Iraq, in the region and throughout the world.

In the wake of a US (and Coalition) withdrawal

from Iraq, the country would become an Iranian-Syrian-controlled base for global jihad. Battle-tested, heavily armed terrorists, cocky after their victory over the Great Satan, would use Iraq as a stepping-off point for attacks throughout the region and world.

Iraqis who worked with Coalition forces will likely be killed, arrested and tortured by their new mafia-like terror masters.

Surgery - necessary or elective

A man has pains in his arm. The doctor examines the person, and tells him that he has cancer. The recommendation is amputation. The person goes to a second opinion, and a third opinion, and all concur that amputation is necessary. Some friends say not to amputate. The patient agrees to the surgery in order to save is life, relying upon medical opinion, not his friends' advice.

After the surgery the arm is examined in the laboratory. The determination is that the pains were not related to cancer, and that the amputation was unnecessary.

A Republican would say that we can make decisions only on the basis of knowledge and intelligence at the time. We cannot make a decision based on intelligence in the future, for waiting can be fatal. All decisions are based upon probabilities. This is how human beings operate.

A Democrat would say that he should have

listened to his friends. The surgery was a surgery of choice, not of necessity. After all, doctors recommend surgery in order to profit. Indeed, when my grandfather was in the hospital, the doctors recommended surgery. My uncle asked the doctor if it is possible for my grandfather to recover without surgery. The doctors said yes, it is possible, but they recommend surgery. They did not operate, and my grandfather died.

This is the situation with the Iraqi war. All professional advice said that our country was in grave danger from the situation in Iraq, and military action was necessary to defend our country. This was the Republican position. The Democrats said that you cannot trust professional advice. After all, we went into Iraq because we wanted to profit from the oil. We could have waited (remember the advice my uncle gave - to wait!). The Democrats said the Iraqi war was a war of choice.

My dear reader, you have to decide whom to vote for. I support the Republicans who act based upon the best advice available at the time. Others support the Democrats, who say we cannot trust professional advice, but instead must confer with our friends and allies and do as they suggest.

A person visits a doctor. After examining the patient, the doctor tells the patient that he has a very serious problem. Historically, many people with this problem have died from the disease. Furthermore, death was sudden rather than gradual. Although we cannot say what will happen, the prudent course of action would be to focus on this problem.

"Wow!" exclaims the patient, "What do you suggest I do, doctor?"

The doctor explains that the patient must focus attention on this issue, and act with the goal of survival. In order to accomplish a goal, we must clearly articulate the goal. We must think rationally and try to minimize emotions. We must bear this goal in mind while we study and think about what we can do.

Although we all can agree that this is sound prudent advice, unfortunately too many people do not act this way, succumbing to emotions from themselves and their friends.

Decline and Fall. When the American Empire Goes, It is Likely to Go Quickly

Professor Niall Ferguson from Harvard wrote a long serious article in the current issue of *Foreign Affairs*. The article is entitled, "*Decline and Fall. When the American Empire Goes, It is Likely to Go Quickly*." Ferguson is a noted historian and speaker. We must take him seriously, and not dismiss him as a kook.

The American people must understand and accept that we are faced with a serious problem that can result in the quick destruction of our country. Historical studies show that this is likely. We must act like the above medical doctor suggested to his patient. We must clearly state that our primary goal is the survival of our country, and then do what we must towards this goal.

As an example, let us consider the current health care debate. Both sides have it wrong. The Democrats say we need this revolutionary proposal in order to make it possible for more people to have necessary health care, claiming that lives and money will be saved. Republicans say the huge costs will be borne by our grandchildren. The reply is so what, if we can make ourselves healthier it should not matter if our grandchildren will pay. The very serious mistake both sides are making is ignoring the primary issue, which is the survival of our country. Democrats must understand that if the Ferguson collapse takes place, the health care of our people will be far, far worse. That is, their plan may result in far greater danger to the health of Americans. Republicans fail to mention the real danger to our very society because of this plan.

What we must all do immediately, in view of Ferguson's article, is to initiate impeachment proceedings against President Obama, based upon "Treason, Bribery, or other High Crimes and Misdemeanors." These proceedings will focus national attention on the Ferguson problem. Congress people can vote against impeachment if they choose, but the hearings should take place in order to refocus national attention on our primary goal, which is the survival of our country and way of life. There are minor issues, as the only clear evidence we have of Obama's birth is a newspaper account, which is not a legal document, or other flimsy evidence.

We impeached President Clinton based upon nonsense that he was fooling around with the girls. What we are now faced with is far more serious that requires strong action.

Let us all work together doing what we can. We are faced with the collapse of our society. We need immediate action. Impeachment is the way to start.

I wish us all good luck, and hope that our great country survives and that our grandchildren will inherit a successful society.

Evaluating a Supreme Court Nominee
America was founded on the basis of the humanitarian ideals of the ancient Hebraic Law as expressed in the Hebrew Bible and rabbinical rulings. The Bible states in *Leviticus 19:15* (my free translation): "You shall not pervert justice by having empathy for the poor or glorifying great people; instead, you shall judge your countrymen with justice."

Elena Kagan's ringing endorsement of Constitutional interpretation demanding "special solicitude . . . for the disadvantaged" means she will not judge her fellow Americans with justice.

Another important verse is *Deuteronomy 16:20*: "You shall pursue justice justice in order that you shall live and inherit the land that God your God gave you." The word "justice" is repeated, to stress that there are two sides that the judges must consider. The reason why we need judges and justice is in order to live. Without justice, a society cannot survive. Since there are questions about Kagan's judicial fairness, appointing her as a Justice will put the survival of America in jeopardy.

In addition to the above basic principles, we need to examine Kagan's qualifications. A university professor receives tenure only if the professor has published a sufficient quantity of formal publications. According to the official *Questionnaire For Non-Judicial Nominees*, Kagan listed her formal publications on only one page. This is not sufficient for tenure at a prestigious university like Harvard, suggesting impropriety that we, especially Harvard professors, should investigate.

According to *The Washington Times*: "We know she is willing to undercut First Amendment free speech for political purposes. Ms. Kagan argued before the Supreme Court that the law should be read to allow the government to prohibit the publication of political pamphlets." This statement makes her unfit to be a justice!

Another Kagan statement: "Why, in a society by

no means perfect, has a radical party never attained the status of a major political force? Why, in particular did the socialist movement never become an alternative to the nation's established parties?"

This unbridled passion for Socialism is arguably enough to disqualify her from sitting on our nation's High Court!

Disclose Act

Though the so-called "Disclose Act" is being sold by Big Labor as a bill to provide greater transparency, its real intent is to harass and intimidate those who might criticize members of Congress into silence during the midterm elections and beyond.

Big Labor doesn't want us, or anyone for that matter, to be able to inform the American people which candidates stand with them – and which ones stand with the union elite.

But, of course, like all the other insider games here in Washington, there is a big loophole.

You see, Big Labor is exempted.

The so-called "Disclose Act" is too dangerous to ignore.

The Economic Recovery Payment

Here is the wording of this payment. "The Economic Recovery Payment: A one-time

payment of $250 will be made in 2009 to:
Retirees, disabled individuals and Supplemental
Security Income (SSI) recipients receiving
benefits from the Social Security Administration."

Isn't this wonderful! Retirees will get an
additional $250 from the Federal Government!

One minor detail. I had to pay $275 tax on this
$250. Cool! The government wins propaganda
saying they are helping senior citizens, while
getting back more than they give! Since this is the
approach of the Obama administration, we must
be very careful and not trust them with anything
they say!

From my accountant:
I can surmise that $250 of the $275 extra tax
(putting aside the small penalty/interest) relates to
the economic recovery payment; a political spin
by Congress (in my opinion). It was "tauted" as
being non-taxable; hence, not reported to
taxpayers on a tax form. Sure it wasn't taxable
income but it reduces the making work pay credit
dollar for dollar; an answer severely worse than
including it in gross income. You are not alone,
almost all of our clients receiving social security
were not aware of this treatment and didn't report
it to us or couldn't remember receiving it. The
following is a link to the IRS' website on the
taxation of the payment. It looks like you do in
fact owe it so long as you did receive the $250
payment. I'm not sure why the $25 difference
between the economic recovery payment of $250

and the increased tax liability of $275 (again excluding penalties/interest). I'd have to look further into that.
http://www.irs.gov/newsroom/article/0,,id=204468,00.html

Hate

We are all making serious errors in our discussions about Rev. Wright and Sen. Obama. (This was written on 04/22/2008). Obama said he was unaware of the hatred, Wright, the church leader, spoke in church sermons during the decades. Our problem surviving today is dealing with hatred that comes from religious institutions and schools. We cannot win our war against terror unless we focus on stopping the inculcations of hatred in religious institutions and schools.

Obama should have actively fought against Wright. Some say Obama should have left the church. Wrong. A true leader does not solve a problem by walking away. He wants to solve the Iraq mess by walking away. We tried walking away from Hitler, and it made matters far worse.

Sen. Hillary Clinton, on the other hand, is a dreamer. She imagined walking with her daughter under a hail of bullets. A successful leader must be aware of reality and deal with it.

The State Department, under many administrations, is not aware of the reality of hate indoctrination across the world. We never hear pronouncements against teaching hate to young children as a form of child abuse.

The only hope for peace in the world is to overhaul the State Department to make them more aware of the teaching of hatred and to make fighting such teaching the highest priority, more important than negotiations. We need to fire career workers in the Department! We will have to get over this and focus on the true problem in the world, which is teaching hate to young people.

Moral character of politicians

Recent talk is about comparing President Obama with Chancellor Adolf Hitler. At first, this is absurd. Hitler was an evil man, a mass murderer, one who wanted to conquer the world. Obama is a good man who wishes to make the world a better place. However, if we look at Hitler's early years before the Holocaust, we find many eerie comparisons with Obama. Instead of ignoring the comparison, we must face up to the possible dangers to America and deal with them, just as we must face up to the dangers of an accident when we cross the street and so we cross properly.

Both Obama and Hitler were very popular eloquent speakers attracting vast crowds. Both Obama and Hitler desire a New World Order, a one-world government. Both Obama and Hitler work towards complete government control of the means of production. Both Obama and Hitler ignore laws and traditions as they move towards their goals. For example, Obama demands that

Honduras returned the ousted president, in spite of the fact that he is ineligible to be president by ruling of the Honduras Supreme Court. Both Obama and Hitler tell Jews where they can and cannot live; Hitler with the Nuremberg laws, and Obama objecting to Jews expanding "settlements".

The main criticism to Obama is in his health care proposals, with government bureaucrats making decisions affecting the lives of people. Hitler's government bureaucrats made decisions who will live and who will die.

Congressman Frank brushed aside criticism that he is acting like Hitler, saying that he is Jewish. Let us not forget that Jews ignored Jabotinsky's preaching that Jews will die in Europe, saying that they were first and foremost Germans for generations.

Comparing Obama to Hitler is a charge that must be taking seriously in order to prevent possible horrors from developing. In particular, we must not scorn those who make this comparison. Again, we must learn from the Jabotinsky failure, where people scorned him for making the prophecy he made.

Judaism has very important moral messages for today's world. Unfortunately, many educated American Jews erroneously accept Christian values for Jewish values. One example is the Christian value of salvation of the self, which differs from the Jewish value of building society in Israel. Madoff, a Jew, focused on his personal salvation while ignoring his obligations to society.

A basic Jewish value is saving lives, which takes precedence over all else. If a group acted in a fashion that resulted in many lives being saved, no Jew would ever accuse the group saying they could have acted differently and the lives would *probably* be saved. Obama, with the support of the media, is accusing government agencies for actions that resulted in American lives being saved, saying they could probably have saved the lives acting differently. We Jews must break our silence, and educate our fellow Americans to these basic Jewish values.

One reason Obama gives for investigating the CIA is to show the world the great wonderful values of America, that we do things the right way. Jews have to say that the CIA discovering threats and preventing them is a great wonderful value that all Americans should be proud of.

Another example is the idea of a "war of choice". This very idea is contrary to Jewish values. A Jew fights and kills because it is necessary to save his life and the lives of his countrymen. A war is absolutely necessary or forbidden, never a choice.

Obama opposes Jewish "settlements" in Israel. These settlements save lives, as the expulsion of Jews from Gaza proved.

Traditionally Jews have been reluctant to discuss Judaism with others. The time we now live in is very dangerous, and Jews have to do what is necessary, which includes trying to understand Jewish values and discussing them with others.

The President of the United States
I get angry when I hear Blitzer on CNN saying "The President of the United States...". He is not the President! I did not see his birth certificate. He is not the Commander in Chief. Any soldier must show his birth certificate to verify that he is not a Russian spy or a member of a terrorist group. Any solder! Including the commander-in-chief! Newspaper accounts are not the same thing, like that idiot O'Reilly says! I resent being called a "birther". I am angry at the courts for taking so long! I am angry at the Democrats for not properly vetting Obama! I am angry at the newspapers for lying to us!

Obama's actions clearly show he wants to destroy the U.S. from within. This would please the Russians. We caught a lot of Russian spies, but the big fishes are still out there. Destroying the U.S., weakening our war effort in Afghanistan by firing the top general, would make the radical Muslims happy. Obama is acting like a Muslim! Refusing to permit ships to keep the oil spill away from the marshlands is an act of a traitor.

I am angry at the big organizations for not fighting for the truth about Obama.

I am angry at our scientists, supposedly guardians of the truth, for not fighting for the truth about Obama!

I am angry at our Republicans for not constantly fighting every move Obama makes to destroy and belittle America!

I am angry that our leaders not criticize Obama when he makes fun of America!

I am angry at people for being so stupid thinking debt and big government are good, when they are evil and destructive! At least today the Tea Party is fighting for the wonderful principle of small government.

I am angry at our Jewish leaders for ignoring the lesson of the expulsion of Jews from England in 1290 (discussed in more detail below). The expulsion was due to excessive debt. The huge debt Obama is imposing on America will result in another expulsion of Jews. Obama is imposing this debt because he is not an American. He does not understand the principles of American liberty and freedom.

This is the challenge of the day. We are fighting for our survival. Let us be good soldiers, brave and courageous in this very important fight!

"If Obama ... serious impeachment..." Forget the "if". Right now we must impeach Obama or else we all die. Obama is the captain of the *Titanic* moving towards the iceberg. Some see the iceberg and are demanding a change in course. The captain is pushing on. Time for mutiny, get rid of the captain, save the *Titanic*! Impeach Obama, save America!

Look at the Pentateuch and count the verses. If we assume the verse number corresponds to the years since the birth of Adam, we find amazing coincidences. E.g., the verse corresponding to 1948 is Deut. 30:3: "And He will gather you from all over..." corresponds to the year when Israel was established. Now go to the verse corresponding to the year 2008: "He will make you jealous with strangers..." This clearly indicates that President Obama is a stranger, not an American.

There are other verses. E.g., the verse corresponding to 1977 is that Moses will die and Joshua will lead the people. What this means is the transition from the Moses government to the Joshua government. Well, in Israel in 1977 there was a transition from the long time socialist Labor government to the capitalistic Likud government.

Okay, we get the point. Obama is a stranger, not an American.

This numerical coincidence in the Hebrew Bible is amazing, but, of course, merely suggestive.

Passover

When Christians celebrate Easter, they remember the Last Supper, which was the Passover Seder. Jews celebrate Passover to remember the exodus from the slavery of ancient Egypt. We must never forget what caused the tragedy of this slavery. It was caused by debt. The Israelites accrued such large debts that they had to become indentured servants. Their condition was hopeless in ever being able to repay the debt. The Bible tells us over and over again never to forget the exodus from Egypt. We must always remember the unspeakable horror debts can cause.

Passover reminds us of the slavery in Egypt. We must remember the cause - debt, forcing them to become indentured servants. Jews must remind Obama and Americans that debt and big government is the way ancient Egypt was run. Jews believe in weak government. The American Founding Fathers got their ideals of liberty from Judaism. Jews must oppose the evil Democrats. Jews must say Obama's ideals are contrary to Judaism and the American Founding Fathers.

Our nation has increased our national debts by huge amounts, and will continue to increase these debts. The government tells us that it is important for our society to have these debts, for then we will have better health care and other things. Some complain that our children will suffer as they have to repay the debts. They are wrong. We Americans living today will suffer horribly in the near future due to these huge debts.

We all must fight in every way to stop government programs that increase debt. We must oppose all new taxes, and stop funding programs for which we have no money. We have to fight those people who are proud to increase debt and oppose the creation of wealth. We must fight those who preach a better environment at the expense of wealth creation. At this time in our history, the highest priority must be the creation of wealth. We must eliminate all restrictions that try to improve the environment, for otherwise we are doomed. It is sickening to listen to my Senator proudly stating his opposition for drilling everywhere.

We are at war. We either stop taxes, restore the Bush tax cuts, defund the EPA, allow massive drilling and mining, keep people from coming into our debt-ridden country. Or else.

We do not understand the danger we are in, just as the world did not understand the danger from Hitler. Remember, we almost lost the war.

Politicians exhibit lack of thinking
I was very disturbed at President Obama's lack of action during a recent health care summit. Obama sat intensely listening and thinking; however, at no time did he write anything down. No thinking person can attend a meeting where different complicated ideas are expressed without writing them down. It is not true to say that he relies on others. The writing is part of the very thinking process. This shows that Obama is not thinking of

the various ideas and concepts people raised. His full focus and attention was on the goal of advancing his agenda. This is very sad. To be focus only on the agenda and not on any ideas is not the mark of a thinking leader.

Unfortunately, the news media simply reports on what people said, without abstracting and discussing the ideas. The focus is on the number of people who support the idea, not on the validity or reasonableness of the idea. This has to change. Pundits must comment on validity based upon basic principles and verification by examining other situation.

Senator Charles E. Schumer sat, arms folded, intensely focused on what another speaker was saying. Schumer is also an unthinking boor, as he sat without writing anything down. His actions in the Senate clearly demonstrate this.

Princeton Professor Uwe Reinhardt
Today's paper interviewed Princeton Professor Uwe Reinhardt. "Health insurance companies know they have made out like bandits." This means they have done very well financially. It is shocking that a respected professor makes such a blatantly false statement.

Furthermore, he fails to mention the mathematical illogic that insurance companies can include pre-existing conditions without raising rates. He says small insurance companies will be regulated out of business, but fails to blame government illogic. We need to directly forcefully confront falsehoods.

The reporter simply did not understand the professor and wrote false information in the paper, for insurance companies have not done well. She also does not understand the mathematical illogic that insurance companies can include pre-existing conditions without raising rates. She does not understand this illogic because her professor also does not understand it.

Drilling for oil

The Obama administration is poised to ban offshore oil drilling on the outer continental shelf until 2012 or beyond. Meanwhile, Russia is making a bold strategic leap to begin drilling for oil in the Gulf of Mexico. While the United States attempts to shift gears to alternative fuels to battle the purported evils of carbon emissions, Russia will erect oil derricks off the Cuban coast.

Offshore oil production makes economic sense. It creates jobs and helps fulfill America's vast energy needs. It contributes to the gross domestic product and does not increase the trade deficit. Higher oil supply helps keep a lid on rising prices, and greater American production gives the United States more influence over the global market.

Drilling is also wildly popular with the public. A Pew Research Center poll from February showed 63 percent support for offshore drilling for oil and natural gas. Americans understand the fundamental points: The oil is there, and we need it. If we don't drill it out, we have to buy it from other countries.

Last year, the U.S. government even helped Brazil underwrite offshore drilling in the Tupi oil field near Rio de Janeiro.

The current price of oil makes drilling economically feasible, so why not let the private sector go ahead and get our oil?

Racism, freedom and inequality
A columnist wrote a column in the Sunday paper discussing the "mistreatment" of Shirley Sharrod, a federal worker who was fired because of remarks she said. He wrote, "The blame belongs to the media, specifically cable television led by Fox, infamous for faux and biased news." No journalist should ever write such a statement. He should have said something like Fox gave this biased false story, and this other "faux". A simple generalization devoid of details is libel.

We should listen to the 40 or so minutes of Sharrod's speech, for she said some very interesting things. She began thanking the president of the NAACP for being present. When the NAACP president denied listening to her speech, responsible journalists should have immediately pounced on him saying he is a liar, as he was present at the talk.

Sharrod said that her father was murdered 45

years ago by a white man. Authorities never charged the murderer with murder. Instead, they charged the murderer with denying Sharrod's father his civil rights. The Supreme Court threw this out, saying the charge must be murder. This was a genuine act of racism. It is important that we understand real racism in the 20th century. Contrast this to 2008. A Republican woman politician said Obama received the nomination because he is black. Obama responded saying she is racist. Her response was, "I am not racist!" Wrong response! She felt she was speaking the truth, and speaking the truth is not racism! Racism is failing to charge a murderer with murder. She should have denounced Obama for levying this charge! We have to fight false charges!

Sharrod continued, saying how she grew up poor on a farm, and how she hated it. She said the government should do more to help the poor people. She criticized the Bush administration for not doing enough for the poor people.

This is the essence of the Obama policy, to do more for the poor people. When governments give money to various good causes, this money comes from the people. Sharrod wants the government to give more money to poor people. Sharrod wants the government to compel rich people to give money to poor people. I like to give charity and help people, but I want to do it of my own free will, of my own choice. I do not want the government to force me. Sharrod wants

the U.S. government to be like Moslem
governments that compel people to give charity.

Sharrod wants the American government to strive
for more equality, in that poor people should be
better off like rich people. I do not want equality.
I want freedom and inequality. I want to do what I
want. I do not want the government to compel
me. I want to move to green energy because I
want to, not because of government mandates.

Actually, what does it matter? We all agree poor
people need help. Does it matter if they are helped
by voluntary charity or by government help from
taxes? Obama and Sharrod think the poor will
better off by government help. Wrong! A
government can only tax money that exists. To
help people by going into debt is just as wrong as
individuals going on spending sprees using credit
cards getting into debt that they can never repay.
When we give freedom and choice to individuals,
people can create money that currently does not
exist. When people are free to think and act, they
create new technologies and ideas that generate
wealth. America is the richest and most powerful
nation on earth due to the creative genius of our
people. As an example, look at the wealth that
Bill Gates created by developing computers.
Gates created his money. This money did not
exist before.

In summary, the emphasis on equality restricts
creativity and freedom and harms wealth creation,
making people poorer. Less government, less

regulations, less mandates, and less moratoriums will help our country prosper, becoming healthier, wealthier, and wiser.

To rephrase in very simple words: The government takes existing money to help others; while if the government would take less money from people, thereby giving us more freedom, people would create more money than currently exists and the poor would get more. The poor people would get more money if the government taxed less and gave more freedom.

Throughout history, people were ruled by rulers that demanded obedience and control. Throughout history, the state was all-powerful. The rulers claimed divine authority. The first revolution against statism was the Israelite exodus from ancient Egypt. The Hebrew Bible stresses freedom and choice, with minimal government interference. The American Revolution against Great Britain was modeled after Hebraic Law, referring to the Hebrew Bible. One of the major holidays in Judaism is Passover, the holiday of freedom. The emphasis is on asking questions and trying to understand principles. The ideal of freedom is responsible for the success of the Jewish people throughout the millennia. The ideal of freedom is responsible for the amazing success of the American nation throughout the past few centuries.

Let us do all we can to keep the ideal of freedom alive. Let us fight with all we can against people like Obama and Sharrod who wish to impose severe restrictions on our freedom. Let us fight against columnists like the above who want less freedom and more government. Let us get out and vote out the politicians who vote for more government actions. Let us vote in the coming elections for people who will support freedom and liberty!

Robert Byrd

Mr. Mahan wrote a letter to the editor saying he knew Robert Byrd as a child, as they lived nearby. Byrd always encouraged Mahan to study and do well in school. They went to different schools. Byrd walked to school, while Mahan, a black man, was bussed 10 miles. Mahan mentioned Byrd's membership in the Ku Klux Klan, and his strenuous efforts filibustering the 1964 Civil Rights Act. Mahan finished his letter saying that in spite of Byrd's racism, Mahan is happy that Byrd was a liberal. The American people like liberalism.

If we all like liberalism and support politicians who are liberal, including racist politicians, we owe it to ourselves to try to understand what liberalism is all about. It is the government taking money from people, recycling the money and returning part to people, with the rest going to government workers and propaganda, with some necessary government activity. Government workers are not bright, creative people. They just want to continue getting their salaries and pensions. The media just want to get the advertising money from the government. Don't you think you and I would be better off if they money just stayed with us, rather than be recycled? Since governments really want your money, you cannot trust them when they talk about taking your money. When they say they need to raise taxes to pay for the stimulus, they are saying they want to recycle your money.

You and I are smarter than most government workers. We can do better with my money than government workers can. Let us stop recycling money. Let people do what they feel best with the fruits of their labor. Then you and I will be better off.

Bloodletting

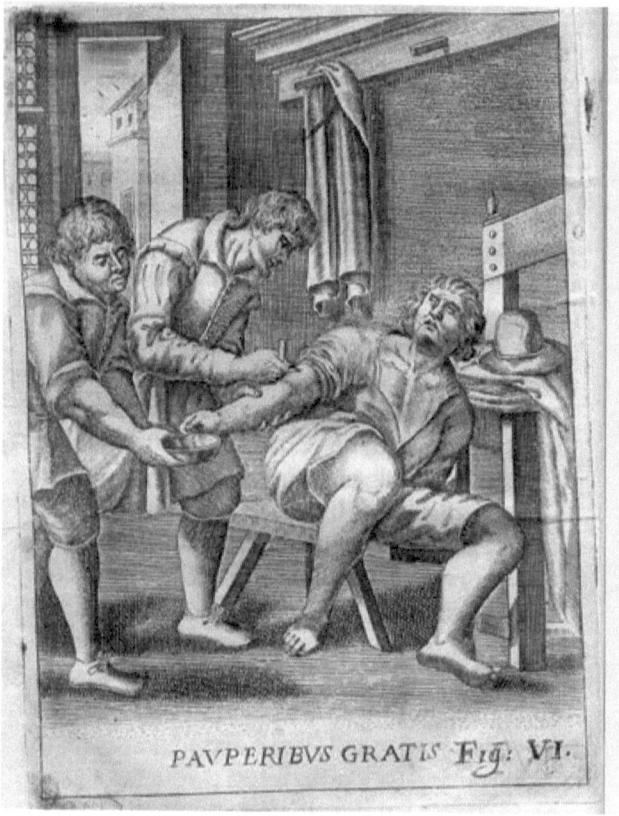

PAVPERIBVS GRATIS Fig: VI.

For many centuries, bloodletting was an acceptable medical practice. World leaders and medical doctors endorsed this practice as a means of helping sick people recover from their illnesses and to resume normal lives. When it did not work, they often recommended a second bloodletting procedure. If the patient died, they said that the ways of the Lord are mysterious; we must pray and have faith.

Why did doctors practice this evil nonsense for so very long? Well, not knowing how to treat illnesses, they wanted to demonstrate active acts of compassion. This satisfied patients, helping the doctors keep their businesses running with steady income streams.

I was once a software developer for Grumman with Secret clearance, working on the JSTARS project, critical for the Iraq war. When I started, I looked at the computer code written by my predecessor. It contained errors in high school trig. I asked my manager how this passed the government inspection. He replied that the inspectors were government employees who wished to keep their jobs. By ignoring faults, they insured their steady employment. This is the real reason for our failures in Iraq, not, as many say, Bush's fault.

This story clearly shows the fallacy of assuming that additional government inspections and regulations will help reducing costly and dangerous errors. Individuals need to take responsibility for their actions. Grumman should have instituted more testing and checking procedures and not relied on government inspections. They did not do this testing, assuming that the "free" government testing would be enough. Our military failures may be attributed to improper reliance on government. Government that is too large is bad for our defense and our economy.

Obama's stimulus program is exactly bloodletting. It is total nonsense, in spite of the many great people supporting it. Now that months have passed with the economy getting worse, we hear talk about a second stimulus. There is no rational basis for it. It runs contrary to the basic principles of our country, USA.

Why not try what we know works - individual actions without the government? Car companies in trouble? Suspend environmental standards for a year. Hiring in trouble? Suspend payroll taxes for a year. Health insurance not working as we wish? Make all insurance tax deductible, not only employer insurance, for a year, eliminate mandates and state differences. Too much carbon dioxide? Have study groups to persuade people and nations, without using government force.

Stimulus money never worked anywhere, at any time. Individual actions do work. They worked building our country from the beginning. When we discuss stimulus money, we do not care what human experience has actually verified. What matters is our beliefs. If Professor Krugman of Princeton University says we need more stimulus money, then we need more stimulus money, in a fashion similar to the great medieval doctors saying people need more bloodletting. If Professor Dershowitz of Harvard University says Obama is acting properly, then Obama is acting properly. We seem to have faith in our great leaders, without thinking for ourselves.

Obama is wrong!
I do not hear this from anyone (almost anyone, I should say). Nowhere can I read such a statement (with a few exceptions).

The Talmud, the is the law of ancient Israel, states that if a court of 23 justices is unanimous in a decision for a death penalty, the defendant goes free. It is not possible to have unanimity, and so one suspects bribery. Likewise, it is not possible for so many pundits on television and in newspaper never to say Obama is wrong. They may say they disagree with him on a small point or whatever, but never bluntly say he is wrong. This means they are dishonest and untrustworthy. This is scary and dangerous for our country.

We can understand that there are no gay people in Iran. We can understand the lack of criticism of dictators in non-Western countries. We cannot understand the lack of severe criticism of the President of the United States. We cannot understand the almost total agreement of business leaders with the Obama economic policies.

We need to fight this attitude. We need to demand people highly critical of Obama to appear on left-wing stations like CNN, to speak without interruption or negative body language. We do not need a Fairness Doctrine to enforce this. We just need to appeal to pundits' honesty. Newspapers need to publish serious articles very critical of the President if they want people to continue to trust the media.

In summary, we can be certain that if all of our leaders are certain about their ideas, then they are certainly wrong.

It is Bush's fault!

"It is Bush's fault!" is the chorus one hears so often when the government is criticized. It is essential for our national survival and interest that we say it is Obama's fault, even if we are not sure. To minimize criticism of Obama is just as bad as not having proper safety procedures in oil drilling. We must quickly and easily criticize the government to help insure proper governing. We must take the attitude the government is wrong until proven otherwise, just as we take the attitude for individuals innocent until proven guilty.

We must understand that we live in a constitutional republic, where the federal government has limited powers and state governments are the final authority. The states have the final say on the constitutionality of federal laws, not the federal courts, for the federal courts are merely part of the federal government.

When New Jersey lost the $400,000 federal money for education, New Jersey has the obligation to criticize the federal government procedures. New Jersey must say, even if they are not sure, that the entire program is unconstitutional, for no federal program can be valid that does not allow for correction of errors.

Once New Jersey declares the law as invalid, the U.S. Supreme Court does not have the authority to overrule the state.

New Jersey must state that the federal government has no authority to grant money for education, as this is not one of the enumerated powers. If we feel that the federal government should finance education, then we need to do things properly, via a Constitutional amendment, not by underhanded executive orders and Congressional actions.

We are headed towards a dictatorship like Venezuela, with powerful national control. The U.S. is built on the idea of powerful states and a weak federal government. We must be vigilant.

The Second Amendment
The purpose of the Second Amendment of our Constitution is to guarantee that we can defend ourselves against the government. The founding fathers were concerned that the government could turn against the citizens, as did the government of France after the French Revolution. It is possible that if the Jews in Germany were not disarmed, the Holocaust may not have happened. This argument may not be valid, but we cannot be sure.

This means that we cannot permit the government to register or license weapons. The government must be totally unaware of where guns are, for this lack of knowledge is the only means citizens can have in defending themselves. Of course, there is no evidence whatever that today we need guns to protect ourselves. If we strongly feel that there is no need to defend ourselves against our government, we can think about abolishing the Second Amendment.

The National Rifle Association is a fine organization. They stress gun training and safety. However, they no not stress the critical point. We need guns not against burglars, but to defend our freedom.

We may look at the steps Israel does to protect its citizens. Parents are required to patrol the schools where their children go to. Here too we could have a civil guard, people with guns and training, to cooperate with the police department to patrol schools and neighborhoods. If we want security, we have to work together.

Some pundits are aghast that people actually want guns to defend themselves against the government. They ask if these people are planning an armed revolution. Sorry, pundits, you miss the point. There is always the possibility that a government will be terrible. The best example is Nazi Germany, where millions of Jews would be alive if Germany had a right to bear arms as we do. We must never give our full and unlimited trust to anyone, including the government.

The Iranian bomb
Iran and the Palestinians earnestly desire a world government under Sharia law. This is what they teach schoolchildren. Israel, *please expose the*

schools books to the world! The trouble is that Obama and Clinton also want a one-world government, a New World Order, and so the U.S. and the Arabs are allies. Israel must expose these terrible world domination crazy ideas! This is why Clinton hints that we must live with an Iranian bomb!

The Greek historian Hieronymus

Although he lived some 2,500 years ago, one can learn much from the Greek historian Hieronymus.

Perhaps no chapter of his history of the ancient Mediterranean world is more interesting than that which discusses Aleris, a city of high culture. Located on the eastern edge of the Mediterranean, Aleris preceded Athens in the arts and sciences, as well as in commerce and agriculture. Hieronymus claims that descendants of exiled Aleri citizens, who had settled in Athens, were the originators of Greek philosophy.

Be this as it may, Aleris was the envy of the Mediterranean. The city often found itself at war with other cities (or city-states). But such was the undaunted courage of her citizens and the advanced state of her military arts, that Aleris readily defeated her enemies on the battlefield.

According to Hieronymus, war in those days was the norm of "international" relations. Pacifism was unheard of. Yet, toward the end of the sixth century before the common era, something unprecedented happened: a peace party called the "Praxites" came to power in Aleris. The peace party constantly magnified the danger of war in order to make citizens feel dependent on their rulers and on the new political order. Hieronymus explains:

"Prior to the reign of the Praxites, the people of Aleris were spirited warriors: proud of their heritage, disdainful of their enemies, superior to all in battle, and second to none in their love of liberty. Fearing only the gods, and believing in a life after death, they were even more disposed to fight and die in defense of their fatherland.

"Now, by means of deception and bribery, the Praxites came to power. The new rulers, consisting of sophists, rejected Aleris' sacred tradition. They realized, however, that they would have to undermine the religion of their people to render them fearful of war, pliable, and dependent on their government.

"Accordingly, the priests were given lucrative government positions to silence them about the warlike intentions of Aleris' enemies. In addition, the Praxites curtailed and eventually eliminated public funds for the religious education of youth. In this way, the anti-traditionalist peace party diminished the likelihood of any popular revolution led by the old religious leaders.

"Recognizing that war fosters public-spiritedness which could threaten their own power, the peace party established schools to foster pacifism. Paltry self-indulgence became the way of life of a once austere city. Gone was the manliness of previous times.

"The new educators of Aleris constantly intoned peace as the highest value. In truth, they were only animated by the desire for comfortable self-preservation. However, by making the city's educators part of the ruling elite, the Praxites had no fear of revolution from that source.

"Meanwhile the Praxites corrupted the Aleris army. Officers were allowed to retire at the age of 40, and with a pension that would make them virtually independent. High-ranking officers were co-opted into the peace party or made the overseers of some commercial or other enterprise. This bound the military to the ruling elite and the existing political order. There was no fear of a military coup.

"To further consolidate their power, the Praxites abolished private enterprise in Aleris. They understood that nothing makes a people more spirited than possessing their own means of livelihood. By making citizens dependent on government largesse, the peace party rendered the people of Aleris servile.

"Consistent therewith, the ruling elite greatly multiplied the number of government jobs. Although most of these jobs had little or no economic justification, they increased the number of citizens who would oppose any change in the political and economic status quo. In this way, the peace party precluded revolution from below as well as from above.

"Despite the veneer of democracy, the peace party thus controlled all the levers of power in Aleris for many years. And since the mantras of 'peace' and 'democracy' were always on the lips of politicians, priests, and educators, the people were held in blissful ignorance of the tyranny that held sway in their city. They believed that their safety and welfare depended not only on the ruling elite but also on the existing form of government.

"When any brave soul spoke up and sought to awaken people from this thralldom, he was ignored or maligned as an enemy of peace and democracy, incarcerated or exiled.

"Of course this condition could not possibly last. Although the rulers of Aleris signed peace treaties with their neighbors, the latter regarded such treaties as preparation periods for the next war, which eventually descended on Aleris like a thunderbolt. These peace treaties only gulled the people of Aleris and made them less vigilant.

"And so, a slavish craving for peace produced only war – the last to be fought by a once brave and noble people."

Jihad

The U.S. must demand that all countries in the world renounce militant Jihad, a doctrine that violates the Universal Declaration of Human Rights.

America has the right to enact laws defining the meaning of the word "religion". A legal religion must adhere to the our laws. Any religion that openly preaches the overthrow of American laws to be replaced by the laws of the religion will be considered as an illegal religion and not afforded any of the Constitutional rights given to members of a religion. In addition, just as American laws demand tolerance towards all religions, a legal religion must be tolerant towards other religions. Finally, any religion that preaches murder or other violence must not be considered as a legal religion. The 1993 Waco raid is a precedent. We need to think if Islam would satisfy these requirements.

The plight of women

Reese Witherspoon spoke to Wolf Blitzer on CNN, talking about the plight of women all over the world. Listening to this, I was horrified by the disinformation. Neither Blitzer nor Witherspoon mentioned the extreme suffering Moslem women suffer!

When they lump Moslem women's problems together with women's problems from the rest of the world, they are falsifying information, hiding the true horror and danger to the entire world from Moslems. Either we understand this reality, or America will be destroyed, just as we did not understand the horror and reality of Nazism until almost too late.

Please open your eyes and open the eyes of the world!

From the media:

The majority of women in Gaza are being denied

inheritance rights though many are not speaking out to tackle the problem.

The *Women's Affairs Center* (WAC) study, Women and Inheritance, found 88 percent of those surveyed claimed to have been denied their inheritance. Around two thirds of those interviewed said they would not request aid to restore their legal rights.

Palestinian inheritance law follows Islamic law, which stipulates that women are only entitled to half the inheritance amount given to men.

For example, if a father bequeaths $1,000 in inheritance to two daughters and a son, then according to Islamic Law (Sharia), the son will receive $500 and the daughters $250 each.

"You can say it's a matter of culture more than religion," Diab Zayed, programs officer at the *Palestinian Working Woman Society for Development* (PWWSD) told *The Media Line*, noting that the problem exists in the West Bank as well as Gaza.

"As a civil organization, we must stand against Sharia," Zayed said.

Executive Compensation Caps

Andrew P. Napolitano wrote that the proposed executive compensation caps violate the Constitution. Furthermore, the judge wrote that the *Troubled Asset Relief Program* for the banks is unconstitutional. This is very serious. Lawmakers take an oath to uphold the Constitution. A violation of the oath is an impeachable offense. The notion that the Supreme Court rules on constitutionality questions is only after the law was passed, and was established by Justice Madison several years after the ratification of the Constitution. *The primary responsibility for deciding constitutionality questions lies with lawmakers.*

Now that Judge Napolitano wrote his opinion, lawmakers are morally and legally bound to explicitly state in any compensation cap legislation why the legislation is constitutional. The pressing need, as the President states, does not justify passing unconstitutional laws. If the need is indeed pressing, Congress should amend the Constitution first, and then pass the bailout legislation.

If the unconstitutional legislation is passed, companies can feel free to ignore it, and pay salaries above the cap. Once the opinion was written down prior to the passage of the legislation, *it becomes unconstitutional without the need for a Court review.*

Torture
The discussions regarding possible government torture of prisoners combined with American values fail to consider critical issues. The primary American value is self-defense, as embodied in the phrase in the *Declaration of Independence,*

"life, liberty, and the pursuit of happiness." If the world properly understands that we will fight using everything we have to defend our country and our way of life, we will be safer.

To understand this basic, very important idea better allow me to give some counterexamples. This pedagogical approach I use with my university students, when I give examples and counterexamples of ideas.

One example is the murder of U.S. Marines in Lebanon in 1983. President Reagan failed to respond to defend the U.S., but instead simply walked away. This sad failure caused America numerous problems later on. As late as today, we have an obligation to track down and punish the killers of our armed forces who were on a peaceful mission.

Another example is Saddam Hussein's shooting at our planes that were patrolling the skies after the 1991 Gulf War. We failed to respond in self-defense after Saddam shot the first plane. This then lead to former Vice President Al Gore to state that Iraq never attacked America, when shooting at the American military is an act of war. Unfortunately, no one mentions these shootings as justification for the second Iraqi war. This is because Americans do not understand what self-defense means.

Moslems wish to impose Sharia law universally. This is a direct attack on our life and liberty.

Sadly, we are not responding to this challenge directly using the hollowed principle of self-defense, saying we will not permit Sharia law to be imposed on our country or on our allies such as Israel. The conflict between Israel and the Palestinians is the not the issue of two states, as most people believe, but the Palestinians' earnest desire for Sharia law.

Let us keep our focus on understanding our basic principles and our founding ideals.

Our country is making a decision that torture is wrong and counterproductive, and must not be used any more. One reason is that it is contrary to our values, and consequently immoral. Another reason is that our enemies may use the idea that we torture as a recruiting tool, with the result that our security will be diminished.

This decision is false for several reasons. Sadly, I have not seen any clear arguments defending torture. The attitude is that torture is absolutely bad. This is a typical error, the notion of absolute, clear black and white, whereas the truth is never absolute.

Let us begin with discussing our values. Our primary value is the preservation of our lives. Self-defense is the highest, noblest of all human values, as well as American values. It is praiseworthy when we kill someone in self-defense. This is what war is all about. We praise our brave men and women who kill to save our country, and use these praises to recruit. We correctly understand that it is them or us.

Unfortunately, some religions express different views. America is not based upon religion, but values, such as those expressed in the Declaration of Independence. Catholics teach that a woman whose life is in danger due to pregnancy should rather die than perform an abortion. The American value is self-defense. The woman must defend her life, taking out the fetus if necessary. Moslems teach that Sharia law must spread to the entire world, and it is good to die for this cause. Americans reject the idea of killing for the sake of an idea like Sharia law.

However, some forms of torture should not be done, namely, those that cause extreme pain or serious bodily harm. These types of torture really do not protect us. We are making a dangerous comparison of these types of torture with other forms of torture that are milder.

Yes, mild torture is fully in accord with American values.

The other argument that we need to remove all forms of torture for our security is false. Our current enemies are not fighting us because we are bad as they see it, but because of their goal of Sharia law.

No Trespassing
As I drive near my house, there are wooded areas

with signs "No Trespassing". I expect that if my friends and I would enter this area, we would not have the Constitutional protection of free assembly. I expect that the police would enforce the laws, and arrest the trespassers.

We seem to fail to realize that the entire area of the United States is a "No Trespassing" zone. No one is permitted to enter the U.S. without permission. People who sneak in and try to work are trespassers, not immigrants. I expect that our police would enforce the laws, and arrest trespassers.

Newspapers have the obligation to present the correct news. When there is a news item about such illegals meeting at various places, they must be referred to as trespassers, not immigrants. Use of the word "immigrant" brings up to our imagination our ancestors who immigrated here, struggled, and finally made it.

The First Amendment to our Constitution applies to citizens and legal immigrants, not to illegal immigrants.

The U.S. Constitution

We do not hear much discussion whether or not we should replace our national Constitution. May we should think about it. Maybe we should replace the Constitution! Many people feel the Constitution should explicitly give the government powerful administrative powers to help alleviate suffering. The goal should be to help the suffering, sick, and poor people. I disagree. The goal should be to encourage the development of the economy, for with a strong economy money will be available to help the suffering.

The best way to help the economy is not by focusing on suffering, but by focusing on freedom. For this end, we need to remind ourselves of our Jewish heritage. Jews escaped from statist Egypt to freedom. The slavery there was caused by debt. We must never forget this lesson that debt causes suffering. The huge debt that Obama is causing will result in horrible suffering for Americans. Jews survived for millennia against powerful destructive forces because of the Jewish ideal of freedom. America was founded on the basis of this Jewish ideal of freedom. America will continue to prosper as long as we remember the dangers of debt and the vital necessity of freedom.

Popular national leaders sometimes lead the nation towards suicide. Hitler was extremely popular. People loved to hear him speak. He led his nation to murder and suicide. The German people failed to understand the great evil of their leader. Great Britain committed suicide in 1945 when Labor nationalized industries, condemning Britain to generations of poverty. British citizens, unfortunately, did not realize the harm and danger of the new government policies. The moral is that citizens have to be aware that popular leaders can do extremely great harm. We all know that when a doctor recommends a serious procedure, one must get a second opinion. We have to take the same attitude towards our leaders. We always have to ask the question, "are the policies our leaders are taking leading to disaster?" We do not ask this question. Instead, we look at polls, or we discuss the policies. Again, we must explicitly ask, what are the possibilities that the policies may lead to disaster and poverty.

We need a Constitutional amendment to address this, for it appears that the Democrats are destroying our economy making all of us poor. This would prevent the government from taking private property except for things like roads, schools, hospitals, military, and such. The government would not be permitted to nationalize an industry, except for war. The government must be prevented from asking banks to make loans contrary to standard banking practices; that is, the government would not be allowed to compel banks to issue subprime loans. Government control of commerce must be limited to safety and maybe standardization (electrical outlets, plane fares based upon distance and seat, etc.) This amendment would strengthen property rights, necessary for America to grow strong and prosperous.

Sarah Palin made a very important statement: "Please, let's not start believing that government is the answer. It cannot make you happy, healthy, wealthy, or wise. What can? It is the wisdom of the people and our families and our small

businesses and industrious individuals."
Regardless of what we think of Palin, all
Americans (including Democrats!) should
enthusiastically endorse these beautiful words.

The threat to our culture comes from within.
Dependency is culture killing. We have to fight
this with a Constitutional amendment.

This is urgent, as most people are stupid and
irrational. They smoke, gamble, drive while
texting, and allow themselves to be influenced by
emotion instead of logic. During discussions,
people frequently reiterate their points rather than
seriously considering the points made by the other
person. They enjoy stories rather than logic based
upon principles. Politicians are people. They are
not logical, are inconsistent, do not focus on basic
principles, desire power rather than the
improvement of society, and full of wrong ideas.
Things are going to get worse, as we ignore
schoolchildren being taught hate and murder, and
we ignore nuclear dangers from people that hate.
For these reasons, it is extremely imperative to
amend the Constitution of the United States.

Article 5 of the Constitution gives states the
power to amend the Constitution without waiting
for Congress. Since the states have this
Constitutional power, they must act responsibly
and use their power correctly. Currently, states are
extremely reluctant to use this power. This is
unacceptable and irrational. The several states
must get together to decide what is the best thing

to do to keep Americans free and prosperous, and to keep government in check. The very least the states must do is to talk about it.

The analogy is police power. Suppose police in a certain region refused to use their power. Crime would increase, and citizens would suffer terribly. However, police do not need to continuously exert their power; instead, people need to know that the police will use their power if necessary. Likewise, states do not have to continuously amendment the Constitution using Article 5; instead, they need to occasionally use this power so that all government officials would understand and respect this power and be more modest in their actions.

Criminals must not be permitted to teach schoolchildren.
The law in New Jersey prohibits criminals from becoming teachers. This is a good law. I do not want criminals teaching my children. The federal government is changing this, and is going to force NJ to permit criminals to teach young children. This is done not by an act of Congress or by an executive order by the president, but by a directive by a regulatory agency, the EEOC, saying that refusing to hire criminals is discrimination.

The only way to fight this is by changing the Constitution. We need to pass amendments that limit the power of the federal government when states disagree. If Arizona wants to limit immigration, the federal government should not be capable of stopping them. If states pass a law based upon a referendum, federal courts should not be capable of stopping this.

We do not have much time. We need to act quickly. Let the states get together and change the Constitution to restrict the power of the federal government and the federal courts. I am scared of having criminals in our schools teaching our children. I am scared that this is being done by a federal regulatory agency with no input from voters.

Even if the EEOC does not mandate criminals teach children, the mere fact that currently they have the power to do this is unacceptable. The answer is not to file lawsuits, for this process is too slow and unreliable. The only way is to constitutionally prevent government agencies from doing these types of things. Our fear of having a Constitutional convention is destructive to the future of our country!

Exodus from Egypt
In spite of scorning Judaism and Jews, the American founding fathers emulated the basic principles of Judaism as expressed in the Hebraic Law. Judaism began with a bloody revolt against statist Egypt. The new society was based upon limited government, with justice. The American Revolution was also a bloody revolution against a statist government. Many American ideals were taken from Judaism.

J. Berman made an interesting point in his 2008 book "*Created Equal*", p. 102. The ancient Israelites had a law that all debts were released every seven years. This is called *Shmita* or the *Sabbatical Year*. "This insures the preservation of a relatively homogeneous society from an economic standpoint. Debt release is depoliticized and placed in the realm of mutual responsibility between members of the brotherhood, serving as a catalyst for the forging of a society with no references to class distinctions."

Lou Dobbs said something similar on an evening CNN news show.

If the government released all owners of mortgages from their debts, our society would be freer, without class distinctions based upon economics. It would cost less than the present plans.

Voting
We must stop focusing on what the candidates say, or other attributes they may have. Instead, we must focus on their basic attitudes and goals. We want someone with a positive attitude, one who encourages individual initiatives, and one who will work to reduce government control and corruption. We want someone who wants to keep America secure and strong, with the emphasis on America.

What would America be like if one of the

candidates became President? We must think about this important question.

If Obama is elected:
1. He would raise business taxes and make the economy worse, as President Hoover did.
2. He would focus on appeasement, as England appeased Hitler, and make the world more dangerous.
3. The government would become much more socialistic, with the focus on helping people (this sounds to me like welfare), and a lack of freedom for business. This would result in the destruction of the economy, business, and personal freedom.

If McCain is elected:
1. Hatred of groups of people in America would continue, with the losers not accepting the election.
2. The economy would be bad, but will recover in a year or two, with the government encouraging business.
3. Corruption will be reduced. For example, Gov. Palin fought Republican corruption, and negotiated a treaty with another country (Canada) for an energy pipeline.
4. America will work for national energy and financial independence and national pride, leading to healthier people and better living for all.

Times Square bomb attempt
Faisal Shahzad is a soldier, an enemy combatant, fighting a war against the U.S. No one seems to speak this truth. This is because of a profound

misunderstanding. Imagine a Nazi young man coming to America during the war. Take your imagination further thinking that he became a naturalized citizen, swearing allegiance to the U.S. Later on he detonates a bomb in a public place. He would be tried and convicted as a soldier in a war, since he was originally a German resident and a Nazi. The difference between the imagined situation and the current situation with Shahzad is that the imagined situation involved America in a war that Congress declared, while today Congress did not declare war. The concept is that war involves countries. During World War II, a state of war existed between the U.S. and Germany. Shahzad was born in Pakistan, and there is no state of war between the U.S. and Pakistan. For this reason, we look at Shahzad as an individual, someone who may have gone off the deep end.

The dangerous misunderstanding is that Islam does not view states the way Americans and Europeans do. We view the world as divided into nation-states. Islam views the world as all people are either Moslems who accept Islam, or those who reject Islam. They declared war centuries ago against all non-Moslems. Moslems consider themselves actively engaged in war against the West. Since they have declared war, the rules of war must apply even if we have not declared war.

Any Moslem who attacks an American must be considered a war prisoner, and confined until the duration of the conflict. Such people must be held as prisoners following the Geneva conventions, without any trial or specified release date.

Our individual responsibility is for self-defense. The rules of war are for our own good and self-defense. If our government releases prisoners of war before the end of the conflict, it puts all of us in serious danger.

What we can do while the prisoners are held is to educate them to American principles of freedom, and to teach them the evils of Islam that their religious writing discusses. We must teach them it is evil to kill non-Moslems. We must teach them it is evil to kill themselves, and they will certainly not go to Heaven. That's it. We keep them in military prisons, and work to educate them. We treat them the way we treated captured Nazis during the war.

Collapse of Industrialized Civilizations

This is very scary. We need to think seriously about this, and how to deal with it. We have a situation where wealthy and powerful people are actively working to destroy our civilization, without regard to the horrible loss of life that would result. Their goals are identical to the goals of radical Moslems, who want to create a new world order, a one-world government, based upon Moslem law.

We must not ignore this, but think carefully about it. It sounds crazy, but so did *Mein Kampf*. We ignore these things at our extreme peril.

Motor Vehicle Traffic Crashes

Very many of us are very angry at our failures in Iraq, and the large number of Americans who have died. This is a noble sentiment, to express concern for death and injury. My question is why is the focus only on Iraq, and not on the much larger cause of death and injury, which are traffic accidents.

Here are numbers. As of April 13, 2007, at least 3,297 members of the U.S. military have died since the beginning of the Iraq war in March 2003, according to an Associated Press count. 3297/4 is 824. In 2005, there were 43,443 fatalities, with 748 in my state, New Jersey. Corzine was Governor. This means that the number of fatalities in New Jersey in 2005 is almost the same as the number of Americans who have died in Iraq in 2005. In 2006, there were 770 fatalities in New Jersey.

If we are so angry with President Bush for the Iraq war, why are we not angry with Governor Corzine for not making serious efforts to use modern technology to save lives? We all know that the Governor has many responsibilities. The very highest priority must be the saving human lives. The highest priority of a government must be the physical safety of the citizens.

Mr. Imus was fired from his popular radio show after making a racist and sexist slur about the basketball players on air. However, Imus did hurt anyone physically. Corzine is partially responsible for 770 people dying in 2006.

Let us see what the Hebrew Bible states. Deut. 22:8, "If you build a new house, you shall build a guard rail for the roof so that you shall not have any blood on the house if someone falls from it." This very clearly states our moral obligation to wear seat belts while driving, and helmets when riding bikes. The Governor permitting people to ride cars without seat belts means that their blood is the Governor's responsibility.

Abolish all tolls in the state, as they cause accidents. Raise money by gasoline tax and a tax on trucks based upon logs. This is done in Georgia. We should study what the state of Georgia does, and do the same here.

Put cameras everywhere, to monitor speed, following too closely, excessive lane changing.

I remember in the 1970's in Israel many people died on the main road between the principal cities of Haifa and Tel Aviv, in head-on collisions. People blamed the drivers. Eventually they put in a concrete barrier, and these horrible collisions stopped. This proves it was not the drivers' fault!

Maybe we should put barriers prevent lane changing on our roads. The accident that hurt the Governor was due to a vehicle that changed lanes!

Let us stop blaming the drivers, like one

columnist saying that pickup truck drivers are very aggressive. Let us use high tech to make the roads safe.

During the first Gulf War, we used JSTARS planes to monitor vehicle traffic in Iraq. This is a radar system that can view every moving vehicle in the country and keep track of it in the computer system. Why hasn't Governor Corzine bought a JSTARS plane, and used it to save our lives?

Yes, our governor was in severe pain on life support. At least he is alive. Not so for 770 residents, who lost their lives in 2006.

I hope that during the months when Governor Corzine recuperates from the injuries, he will spend some quality time thinking what New Jersey can do the make our state safer. Now, however, that he is out of office, it is clear he never spent any time making our state safer.

Stay away from a false thing
Judaism has important messages to the world. Freedom, which means *individual*, not government, ownership of means of production. The Hebrew Bible states, "Stay far from a false thing." Jewish scientists have the moral obligation to speak out clearly against the lies that carbon dioxide is warming the earth. Israel must directly challenge and fight U.S. President Obama's plans concerning carbon dioxide production. This is our responsibility as Jews.

Citizens must anticipate political actions
Citizens must anticipate political actions their
leaders will take. There are three principles we
can use to help us. One is to study the politician's
history, and assume the person will continue
acting in the future the way he/she acted in the
past, regardless of changes in present behavior or
formal statements. The second way is to
understand public opinion, and to assume the
politician will follow. The third way is to look at
big money possibly influencing the politician,
without waiting for formal verification. Here are
examples how informed citizens should react.

History. Rule one is to look at the person's
history. This actually is an extension of the rule
that we need to look at a nation's history in order
to understand what a nation will do. Barack
Obama spent 20 years in a radical church. During
the campaign, the proper reaction of citizens
should have been to assume Obama would
continue following the ideals of this church in
spite of his formal denials and rejection of the
church. What is unsatisfactory is the fact that the
media accepted Obama's denials. The media
violated this rule.

Public opinion. Rule two is to look at public
opinion. This is something we all do, which is
good. However, we must remember that there are
three rules, not one rule.

Money. The third rule is to look at possible
money. We know there are powerful international

interests in a one-world government. Saudi
Arabia is dedicated to the principle of a single
world government, and spends vast sums of
money towards this goal. Mr. Soros also spends a
lot of money towards this ideal. This goal is
contrary to the U.S. Constitution, according to
which our national government is supreme, not
any other body like the UN. When we find
American leaders supporting actions contrary to
the Constitution, and making false statements that
their actions are in accord to the Constitution, we
can assume this is due to monetary influence,
even if we cannot find any such evidence. This
may explain the Mayor Bloomberg's surprising
approval of the mosque near the site of the World
Trade Center.

The Arab Lobby Rules America

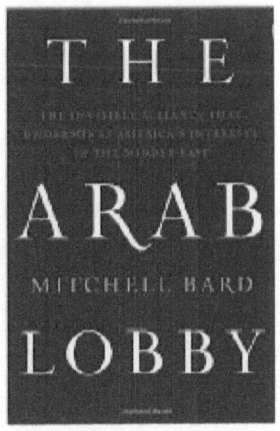

Professor Alan M. Dershowitz made this point in his new book, *The Arab Lobby Rules America.* His point is Arab lobby is one of the strongest in America, stronger than Israel's. He states, "One of the most important distinguishing characteristics of the Arab lobby is that it has no popular support. The Arab lobby in general and the Saudis in particular make little effort to influence popularly elected public officials, particularly legislators. The primary means by which the Saudis exercise this influence is money. They spend enormous amounts of lucre to buy (or rent) former state department officials, diplomats, White House aides, and legislative leaders who become their elite lobbying corps. Far more insidiously, the Saudis let it be known that if current government officials want to be hired following their retirement from government service, they had better hew to the Saudi line while they are serving in our government." The methodology employed by the Arab lobby is thus totally inconsistent with democratic governance, because it does not reflect the will of the people but rather the corruption of the elite.

Our responsibility as citizens is to be aware of these influences and act accordingly, without waiting for formal proof. Let us remember that no government can completely eliminate wrong things, like money influencing policy, and consequently it is our individual responsibility to be alert and vigilant, and to properly understand these things.

3. Economics

The Great American Bubble Machine

The Madoff scandal is an opportunity for the growth and spread of worldwide anti-Semitism. One question we must ask ourselves is could we have stopped this earlier? Another question we must ask ourselves are there other similar scandals that require Jewish whistle-blowers?

Rolling Stone Magazine wrote an article about Goldman Sachs Corporation. The article originally appeared in RS 1082-1083 from July 9-23, 2009. The article stated that GS succeeded over the decades to change and evade laws designed to protect investors, and so stealing vast sums of money, far larger than the Madoff scandal. It is vital that Jews become at the forefront of exposing GS for the evil they perpetuate. It is especially that the Israeli government takes the lead in exposing this scandal. We Jews must realize that we must be proactive, or else they will hit us very, very hard.

Let us do what we can in time to save ourselves.

Comparing capitalism and socialism

To solve problems and to optimize our national

survival we need to use our learned human ability for rational thinking. We must clearly state and phrase the issues, understand and apply the relevant principles, and examine similar situations in other times and places for verification of the ideas. Thinking is complicated. If we gloss over any of the above steps we can easily arrive at false and dangerous conclusions. We all must insure that we personally understand the various complex steps and approve of them. We must be careful not to fall for slogans by popular leaders.

Thomas E. Woods Jr. wrote in the *Intercollegiate Review*, Fall, 2009 an article entitled, "*Warren Harding and the Forgotten Depression of 1920*". Harding cut the budget, reduced spending, taxes, and the debt, with the result that the depression lasted only one year. In 1920 unemployment was 12%. By 1923, it was 2.3%. We unfortunately have forgotten about this real economic miracle.

When FDR came into power, America was hit with another depression. FDR did the opposite of what Harding did. Burton Folsom Jr. and Anita Folsom write a column in the *Wall Street Journal* on April 12, 2010 that FDR did not end the Depression.

What our economists and political leaders have not done is to take the above facts to a logical conclusion. Imagine that Harding was President instead of FDR. The Depression would have been over in 1930. Within two years we would have full employment. The booming times would encourage trade with Europe and, especially Germany. There would have been no need to start the war. The Holocaust, along with the scores of millions of other deaths, would not have happened. This clearly means that FDR's policies caused World War II.

President Obama is following the exact recipe for dealing with unemployment as FDR did. We can therefore expect the same results. We can expect the current recession to last a decade to be followed by a world war.

Americans failed to vigorously oppose FDR's socialist policies. Americans failed to insist on adhering to the principles of economic freedom our founding fathers expressed. Americans failed to demand that FDR not act violating the spirit and letter of the Constitution, foolishly depending on the justices of the Supreme Court. This sad failure resulted in WW II. To this day, too many people are silent about FDR, instead of denouncing him for his horrible policies that resulted in such vast loss of life.

We have to study the works of Woods and Folsom, mentioned above, in order to know how to act today. Since Obama is acting like FDR, we must oppose Obama vigorously. We must fight all the stupid ideas the Democrats put forth, if we are to prevent a world war. Remember, the huge debt the Germans had caused them to start the war.

Obama wants people to love him and to love

America. What is the source of the hate? The answer is that America was founded on the Jewish ideals of individual freedom and limited government. Strong governments hate freedom-loving people. This is the reason for the curse of anti-Semitism. The reason Arabs hate American, and try to kill Americans, is because Arabs want everyone to follow Sharia law and not be free to follow their conscience. Israelites escaped from statist ancient Egypt for freedom with limited government. Americans revolted against Great Britain for the same ideals of freedom and liberty.

There is a lot of confusion about the nature of capitalism, and a lot has been written on this subject. Let us not think that capitalism is simply the focus on profit. Instead, capitalism is the focus on the individual doing his best to accomplish his goals. Some people are immoral, and lie and steal in order to accomplish their goals. To reduce this harm, we need government. The discussion here is about a capitalist government, not anarchy. However, if the government is too strong it will also lie and steal in order to accomplish its goals, for the government is composed of people. This is why we need a limited government, such as the American government based upon the Constitution.

A person in a capitalistic society may have goals to improve the society. Contrast this with the person in the socialistic society, who is mandated to working to improving the society. A self-motivated person accomplished far more than a person ordered to do something.

Progressivism

The goal of politics is action to improve our security and economy. We tend to confuse politics with sports or litigation, where the goal is winning. We must keep our focus on our true goals. In order to maintain this necessary focus, we should reiterate our goals, and constantly examine political statements and actions in this light. We need to clarify both the logic and empirical and historical confirmations. An example of a common error is Alan Greenspan's statement that increased taxes are needed in order to increase government revenue, when over three decades of fiscal data contradict this. People need to understand the truth that lower tax rates increase government revenue.

The question of Democrats or Republicans in the coming elections must not override this logic. Many people are convinced that Progressive ideas are harmful to our economy and indeed to our security. Many journalists refuse to properly discuss clear evidence against Progressivism.

Several noted billionaires are Harvard University dropouts. Let us not err saying that they felt people do not need higher education, because they do not feel this way. Instead, they object to Professor L. Summer's teaching that government is necessary for prosperity and the more government the better we all will be. Bill Gates and other wealthy people feel that without government they will figure a way to make money, and they are right. They know universities are teaching false doctrines. We need to debate these professors, challenging them for their false ideas of Progressivism and Keynesian economics.

Let us not say the Tea Party consists of angry, emotional people. Instead, they are rational, intelligent people who disagree with ideas many people unfortunately have. When we characterize someone as angry, saying anger is the primary quality, we are saying the person is primarily emotional. This certainly is not true for members of the Tea Party movement, who are primarily logical and concerned about America's future.

Foreign policy and business

It is imperative for the sake of world peace that the U.S. State Department focuses its priorities on encouraging business partnerships between neighboring countries, especially countries that are not friendly to each other. We must emphasize what we do best, and that is business.

We can succeed in Iraq only when we find a successful business model that has the promise of prosperity for the poor Sunnis, who feel threatened by the rich Kurds and Shias. Legal talking and diplomatic negotiations are not as important as business.

The model is Israel and Jordan, who have a positive business relationship in spite of formal animosities.

Israel's withdrawal from Gaza can succeed only if America works to help the Arabs in Gaza develop a tourism industry that Israeli and American can partake. If the Jews and Arabs cannot be business partners, they will continue killing each other, and eventually Israel will reconquer Gaza.

Israel is asking money from America to finance the Gaza withdrawal. America must make it clear that America is interested only in helping Israel and its Arab neighbors do business together.

Debt. I think this is one of the most critical issues Jews face. Debt caused centuries of hatred and anti-Semitism. The present debt level scares me. We Jews must write and spread the word about the horrors of debt. If we do not learn the lesson from 1290, Jews may find themselves expelled from the U.S. Fortunately, in this case, we have where to go - to Israel. We have to start preaching about debt.

The 1984 DVD "*Heritage: Civilization and the Jews*" by Abba Eban made the point that Jews played a unique role in that era. They were not allowed land, could not farm or enter crafts, and so had no choice but to engage in commerce. Since Jews are very hospitable to each other, it was easy for them to travel vast distances. Jews uniquely supplied the money necessary for the European economy in the Middle Ages. The increase in money due to Jewish activity resulted in building booms, which lead to huge debts. When the debt load reached a critical stage, where the rulers could not repay the debts, they attacked their debtors, the Jews, killing and expelling them.

The lesson we must learn is the tragedy and suffering the Jews felt for the ensuing centuries was a result of debt. This means that we must be afraid, be very afraid, of debt. A case can be made that the Nazi Holocaust and World War II was the result of huge debt. The implication is that the debt load that the American government is taking upon itself for the purposes of social programs may result in war, horror, and millions of deaths.

The expulsion of the Jews from England in 1290

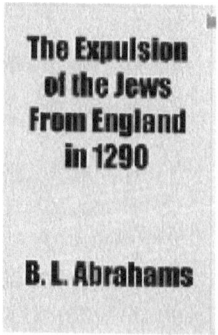

The Expulsion of the Jews From England in 1290

B. L. Abrahams

This book, by B. L. Abrahams, clarifies the debt issue. In spite of the voluminous writings on the origins of anti-Semitism, little has been said about issue of debt that caused modern anti-Semitism starting with the expulsion of Jews from England.

We have a moral obligation to clarify and explain this to the public. We must understand that it is better for a society to forgo social programs and benefits but to stay debt free.

Of course it has been well researched. My point is not the details of this historical event, but that debt caused the expulsion and subsequent hatred of Jews for centuries. People miss this point due to the large amount of facts of that era.

My point is that we have to understand the horrific consequences of debt. It is our solemn obligation to properly clarify this point today. We must shout out as a prophet decrying the dangers to our country by our huge debt. We must stand up as did Nathan the Prophet and say to the leader of the world, "You are the man who is leading the world into ruin by debt!" Say this based upon facts. We must condemn world leaders. We must educate the public on the extreme dangers, including terrible wars and hatred, which debt can cause. We must build the case step at a time so that the public can understand and act to stop this debt curse.

The Bible and taxes
Many Americans are very happy and emotional about the Obama victory. People are happy about Obama's pledge to roll back the Bush tax cuts, feeling that the effective tax increases will restore prosperity. Although Obama promised not to raise taxes on 95% of Americans, the very idea of rolling back tax cuts means tax increases. These

tax increases on the "wealthy" are good for the country, for they will give the government revenue, so that the government can improve the infrastructure, medical care, and our economy.

Logical analysis, using numbers and historical data, show the very opposite of these utopian claims. Obama has never addressed the specific points, giving reasons why they are not valid. The campaign is over, and we must stop with emotional slogans. We must look at the arguments and demand clear rational thinking. We must be willing to "flip-flop" if the analysis leads to a reverse position. We cannot run the country based on emotion or decisions based upon power and influence ignoring reason.

Since Obama wants to raise taxes, it is instructive to see what the Hebrew Bible says about taxes. The story about the Egyptian enslaving the Israelites begins with (Ex. 1:11), "And they placed upon them tax collectors." *The slavery began with taxes!* Jews are commanded never to forget the lessons of the slavery in Egypt and the redemption from this slavery, and celebrate the Passover festival. We all must never forget how this slavery began with taxes!

The Talmud relates that on the Seder night when discussing the exodus from Egypt, Jews are supposed to eat bitter herbs to recall the bitter slavery. The proper herb is romaine lettuce, for it is initially sweet, but later bitter. The slavery was initially sweet. The government gave sweet deals to the Israelites, but they could not pay back the mortgages. The phrase "Egyptian slavery" is literally translated as mortgage indebtedness to Egypt. This is exactly what is currently happening here in America! The government gave sweet deals to Americans by forcing banks to give loans to poor people unable to return them, with the resulting consequence that many are now slaves to the government, with no where to live! Let us hope we can resolve this without ten plagues hitting us!

Now the government is bailing out the unfortunate. Again, let us look at the Hebrew Bible, at the story of Joseph. There were seven good years, when the government stored grain. Then came seven bad years, a severe depression. The Joseph government bailed out the public, and gave them food and seed. Then the Bible continues saying that the government moved people around the country! This is what is happening here today – people are losing their homes and moving around the country! We should read this story carefully, for it is very relevant!

We hear talk that we should restore the high
Clinton taxes, for times were good then, and we
are now in trouble because of the Bush tax cuts.
The Bible says exactly the opposite, that high
taxes are not good for the country. Ancient Israel
was at its peak during the reign of King Solomon.
He was considered the wisest man in the world.
He built the first temple in Jerusalem. When he
died, the public approached his son Rehoboam,
the new king, and asked that the taxes be reduced.
This whole store is in simple, clear Hebrew. It is
beautiful to read. It is in Kings 1 12.

Here is the story. King Rehoboam said he would
reply in three days to the request for lower taxes.
He conferred with his advisors. The first group,
"wise intelligent" advisors, Solomon's advisors,
advised the king to reduce taxes. This would
please the public, and they would do anything he
wished.

The king then turned to another group, "childish"
advisors, people with whom he grew up. They

advised keeping the Solomon high taxes (as Obama advises to keep the high Clinton taxes). The king heeded the childish advisors. This angered the public. (Once Obama reinstates the high Clinton taxes, the public will become angry, regardless what they say now.) The result was the breakup of the country into a small country of two states with high taxes, and a large country with 10 states. The large country, with lower taxes, became prosperous, with the high tax country becoming poor, even though they had the Temple in Jerusalem.

To repeat, the Bible says that present-day Republicans are wise people for the desire to reduce taxes, and Obama and the Democrats are childish in their desire to raise taxes. The childish folly of maintaining high taxes led to the destruction of the unity of the country. We can expect the same thing today. If Obama keeps taxes high, we can expect states to secede from the United States, as people are already talking about secession.

One lesson is that going back to an earlier high tax government will anger the people, enough to revolt. Let us not forget that America revolted against Great Britain because of the taxes. Solomon was extremely popular, but when the next king wanted to continue the high taxes, it did not work. Clinton was popular, but if Obama continues high taxes, it will not work.

Another lesson is that the way to national

prosperity is by lowering taxes.

For the continued success of our country, success that we always pray for, we must try to reduce taxes as low as we possibly can. We must avoid crossing the threshold whereby raising taxes reduces government revenue. We are very close to this threshold.

The Bible teaches us that people revolt in anger at high taxes. Obama must not count on his popularity to save him from public anger if he raises taxes.

Thelma & Louise

Thelma & Louise is thought of as a 1980s movie, but it actually came out in 1991. It stars Susan Sarandon and Geena Davis as two suburban women – an Arkansas waitress and a housewife – who go on a wild road trip after fleeing from a crime. The movie's tagline: "Somebody said get a life... so they did."

At the end of the movie, Thelma and Louise have to decide whether or not to turn themselves in. They look at each other in the front seat of their convertible Thunderbird as an army of police cruisers closes in on them.

Rather than surrendering to the police, Thelma and Louise make a suicide pact. They decide to "go all the way"... and drive the Thunderbird over the edge of a cliff.

The *"Thelma & Louise"* theory argues that this is what the U.S. consumer is doing: If it's all hopeless anyway, why not "go all the way" and drive over a financial cliff. "Shop til you drop," long an American art form, is being turned into a literal plan.

A psychology of relentless optimism, bordering on delusion, acts as partial explanation. But a nagging question still remained. Where did the money come from?

Or, in keeping with the analogy, how did Thelma & Louise (aka U.S. consumers) actually fund their road trip? From whence came the cash?

The recent boost to retail sales could have come from a surge in Strategic Defaults. A recent article by documented that for every foreclosed house on the market another 5-6 houses are in strategic default.

Assuming their mortgage was the single largest expense in their budget, they suddenly have a lot more spendable money. That additional spending money could account for both the recent drop in credit card delinquencies as well as a recent uptick in retail sales.

All of a sudden, the picture becomes much more clear. Strategic default 'mad money' could well be the fuel consumers relied on to power their ' recovery.'

So what did these millions of debt-besieged homeowners do? They chose the strategic default option, putting credit cards over mortgages... and suddenly had much more money to spend, being free of the odious monthly mortgage nut.

4. Education

These are thoughts on education, based upon my experience teaching and observing.

Education in Afghanistan

Articles in the newspaper about education in Afghanistan omitted a critical point. The primary goal of Moslem teaching is the ideal of universal *Sharia* law, the idea of a single world government under Sharia law. This is similar to many American governments and leaders, who strive for a *New World Order*, a single world government that will deal fairly will all people, working to meet the needs of everyone.

These ideas are very wrong. As I have written in my book *"Teaching and Helping Students Think and Do Better"*,
our goals must be survival and economic growth, with any noble national ideals as secondary goals.

When we substitute the secondary goal for a primary goal, we all lose and suffer terribly.

When we speak about open borders and jobs, we are not focusing on the primary goals of survival and growth. When schools in Afghanistan focus on the need for all to strive and die for Sharia law, they fail to focus on the primary goal of survival.

We must be vigilant and do all in our power to oppose false secondary goals, such as Sharia law and government controls. We need to be rational and examine successful periods in our history and look for the reasons, and try to copy these reasons in the present.

It is vital for our physical and social survival as a nation that we make ourselves aware of the education of school children in Arab countries and act to the very best of our abilities to do the right thing. This must be given the highest priority.

As an example, Hamas slammed the *United Nations Relief and Works Agency* (UNRWA) for proposing a chapter on the Holocaust for middle school students. Hamas said the Holocaust is a lie. We must fight the Hamas. We must fight all teaching of hate, and teaching that ignores the Holocaust.

The same is true in Iraq and Afghanistan. We cannot tolerate teaching hate, for these children, who learn hate in schools, will then carry out their hate against us, killing us.

Communication

To excel at teaching, one must excel at communication. To be a good student, one must also excel at communication, for we teach each other. Communication is essential to intellectual development. This implies that to be a good scientist one must also be a teacher. Consider the 20th century giant, Albert Einstein. Once Einstein was accepted to the *Institute for Advanced Studies* in Princeton, NJ, he ceased to produce anything significant. Note that this Institute is not Princeton University. Einstein did not have any teaching responsibilities. My theory is that he did not have any student contacts.

When one has to understand students' thinking and work towards how to present ideas that they understand, and when one is focused on basic principles striving to convey these principles to students so that they can use them for rational thinking and analysis, then the teacher must be creative to understand the students and grow intellectually. Each student and each class is different. This presents fresh challenges to the professor or teacher.

When I look at our society, with so many smart successful people falling for swindlers like Madoff, when I look at banks acting irrationally succumbing to government pressure to give loans that violate centuries-old banking principles, I wonder why we are so stupid. I cannot change the country, but I can change my students, to help them understand thinking based upon rational principles. This type of thinking is critical for all students, not only science, mathematics, and business.

The difficulty is the improper training in high school, with the emphasis on rote and doing things certain ways without stressing the principles. This represents a failure to communicate the ideas to the students. When the students come to college, not only do we have to teach them the correct way, but also have to unlearn the wrong way.

As an example, consider the idea that a variable represents an abstract quantity. Teachers fail to communicate this. Instead of correctly saying something like "Let x be the number of pounds of peanuts," students say, "x is peanuts," which is a serious conceptual error. The teacher must communicate that the students create the variable x that exists only in their minds. The variable x is not the bags of peanuts lying around, but a mental concept.

Here is an example of communicating principles. If we say $x + 3 = 5$, students will say move the 3 to the right hand side and get $x = 2$. The truth is that 3 is an abstract quantity, and one cannot just move an abstract quantity. Instead, we have axioms. One is the axiom of equality (e.g., $-3 = -3$), and the axiom that two valid equations can be added to yield a valid equation.

In summary, an important principle of communication is to stress the basic principles and logic, giving examples and counterexamples. We need to start from agreed-upon points, and move towards goals while stressing the principles along the way. We are communicating our thoughts, which are based upon principles.

The University News
This was published as a Letter to the Editor in the university newspaper, the *News*.

Reading the discussions in the *News* about the recent visit of Governor Huckabee prompted my thinking. A major goal of a university is the development of students' abilities for critical thinking based upon fundamental principles and correct information. Proper logical analysis of a problem or issue is often lengthy, unsuitable for time-limited verbal communication or brief written newspaper articles. Restricting discussions to fit into such limited formats may lead to wrong conclusions. The solution is to have a webpage with the proper complete discussion, with a committee of professors and students editing responses for logical and factual accuracy, and to remove duplication. Unedited blogs are not useful for this purpose. The invitation of a speaker should include the expectation that the speaker will receive these edited comments and submit a reply. The objection that students were in another room unable to ask questions is not valid, for it is impossible for a large body of people to ask verbal questions under any reasonable time constraint. The only solution is written communication, with the speaker taking time to carefully respond in writing. Today we cannot have speeches hours long, as was the case for the Lincoln-Douglass debates, but we can have long articles in print and on the Internet.

Is it right to discuss in the *News* gay marriage and not to mention the recent student discussions in the *News* on this topic? Professors need to mention previous student comments when discussing with students, but there was no space in the newspaper. Can we speak about the right of a woman to her body and not mention the government prohibition of using one's body and fist to punch someone? It is not different and opposing views that we want. Instead, we want clear, logical, consistent analysis. My classroom experience is that students may make mistakes doing problems by ignoring statements given in the problem. This may be caused by today's attitude of thinking in sound bites, television debates that must fit in between commercial breaks, and limited newspaper space. Restrictions due to time or space on expressions or questions may lead to errors. Fortunately, the Internet gives us all the opportunity to remove these restrictions.

Professors write serious, lengthy articles and books that are peer reviewed. We professors can encourage the next generation to be like us, and to write serious articles that are peer reviewed. We can do this with the help of the Internet. This will help the University become great, and the students more capable of dealing with the difficult challenges they will face in life.

Obama's Lesson Plans

The purpose of education is to help students understand the world and themselves: Western Civilization, the ideals of the founding of our country and the American Revolution, some principles of mathematics and science, and communication (literature and language), and art. We all must keep our focus on this goal. Teachers must pay attention to whether students understand or not. Students have the responsibility for understanding during class, and asking questions if not. Understanding and learning includes review. Homework is review, basic to understanding. It is also critical to discuss the material with others, not only to help the understanding and review, but also to create emotions necessary for retention. When people talk and make eye contact, as opposed to communicating via machines, there are always emotions. For this reason, parents need to encourage children to talk about what they learned, for talking and making eye contact is critical to learning.

President Obama espoused a different philosophy of learning, diametrically opposed to the above ideas. Obama said in his speech to students, "… teachers responsibility for inspiring you, and pushing you to learn." One does not learn by pushing. Some religions teach by mindless rote and review. This is not how we learn today. The teacher must focus on understanding, not inspiring. Teachers must focus on communication, understanding how students think and building from there based upon the principles. I wrote these ideas in my book.

Now that the President said these incorrect words, I have to work extra hard as a teacher to help students unlearn the mistaken ideas Obama mentioned.

Parents' responsibility is not simply to insure students get their homework done, but to communicate to students about their work. If the student knows more that the parent, this is an opportunity for the student to teach the parent, and parents should be eager to learn. The task is to listen, not to "push", as Obama said.

I asked a 6th grade student if he likes homework. "No," he replied. "Why do you do homework?" I asked. "To get a good grade," he replied. My reply was, "You do homework as a review of the material, and review is critical to learning. The entire purpose of school and education is to learn and understand, and homework is part of this. Whatever you do, you must know the goal, the reason. The reason for homework is for the goal of learning."

Obama said, "… the government's responsibility for setting high standards." No, it is the parents' and community's responsibility. If the parents are not interested in high standards, we need to focus on educating the parents to understanding themselves and their community. If the parents are not interested in high standards, the government cannot force them and create the standards.

Here are some more errors in the speech.

- "Pay attention to the teachers." Teachers are supposed to pay attention to students, to see if they understand. Students are to try to learn, not try to pay attention. What does attention mean?

- "Listen to your parents." Again, parents are supposed to listen to their children and guide them, and help them learn.

- "Put in hard work to succeed." This is a meaningless and useless statement. The correct statement should be, "Put in hard work to try to understand what you are learning."

- "You won't love every subject you study." If you dislike a subject, is usually means you do not understand it properly. This may be your fault, or the teacher's fault, but rarely because of the subject.

- "Not every homework assignment will seem completely relevant to your life…" Homework is not important because of relevance, but as an extension of the class, as a review and as a check of understanding. If a student is concerned about relevance, the time to raise this question is in class, not at homework.

- "What's your contribution going to be?" Irrelevant question. The correct question is "What are your goals?" I ask students what is the most important thing about driving, next to safety, which is first. The answer is knowing where you are going. If you know how to steer and use the gas, it does not do you any good if you do not know where you are going. We need to focus on our goals, not on our contributions.

- "Don't be afraid to ask questions." Where did the idea of fear come with questions, unless teachers discourage questions? Instead of telling students not to be afraid, we must tell teachers not to be afraid to encourage students asking questions.

There is another major conceptual error in the President's speech. One thing critical for learning is understanding one's body. In particular, sleep is critical. Sleep-deprived students fail in proper learning. During the night, thoughts that happened during the day are solidified in the brain. Without proper sleep, the day's learning will be disorganized. I tell my students to try to get a good night's sleep before examinations in order to get better grades. In addition to getting enough hours sleep, it is important to have a regular schedule so that the sleep is better. Parents and teachers must understand this, and convey this message to students.

When Obama proudly says at the beginning of the speech that he got up at 4:30 in the morning, and was very tired, he conveys the precise opposite message, a very destructive message. Many deadly accidents are caused by sleep deprivation. The President should encourage Americans to set proper sleep as a major priority in their lives.

It is scary that the President of the United States could make a speech to our students that contains so very many serious pedagogical errors. *One conclusion is that we must close the Department of Education, for we can blame them for preaching bad ideas.*

Obama said, "Make us all proud." Sadly, I am not proud of President Obama!

Gifted children

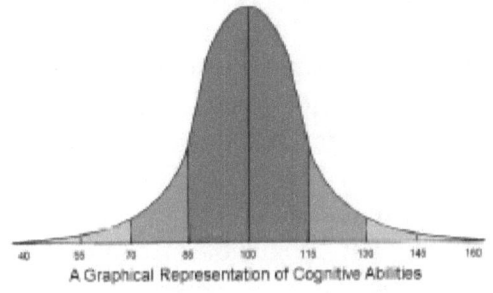

A Graphical Representation of Cognitive Abilities

Americans have a fetish for equality. The government makes major policies, imposing severe hardships on people, towards the aim of equality. We have it all wrong! People are not equal! The goal should be freedom. Let all of us do our best. If we permit excellence and permit the superior people to have the freedom to do what they desire, all of us will be better off.

This incorrect attitude affects our education. We spend vast sums of money helping the disadvantaged in our efforts towards equality, while neglecting spending money helping the gifted. We need to focus vastly more resources in helping gifted students excel. The future of our country will be made by the gifted. We should be very happy to help the gifted excel, for this is our future! See *Under-Representation and Gifted Education*, **Gifted Education Press Quarterly,** Fall 2010, by Donna Y. Ford.

We need to emphasize freedom, not equality. We need to stress the gifted, not the disadvantaged.

The superintendent at a school meeting proudly stated that the school has many gifted students who go to universities before graduating high school. The attitude of the superintendent was that the school deals with all types of students, including the gifted. This is the approach American educators take. This is based upon the belief that we must exercise equal efforts to all. This belief is actually not a genuine American belief. Americans believe in equal opportunity for all, not equal efforts for all.

The best approach, both for the benefit of the

students and for our country, is to focus primarily on the gifted, with, of course, not neglecting average students. The emphasis of our education systems should be the gifted. There are several reasons for this.

One reason is that the future of our country depends upon the gifted students. Our prosperity, health, and happiness depend upon the success of gifted students. We should focus our primary efforts on the most productive and beneficial. This will give us the most bang for our bucks.

Another reason is that serious effort towards the gifted students will benefit all students. One major problem in our schools is boredom. Schools teach mathematics by telling students what to do. The student must memorize a large number of arbitrary rules that seem pointless. Many articles are written what to do about this problem.

Consider the situation where the teacher talks to the gifted student, explaining the basic principles and logic of the subject. The others will then try to understand and be interested. What the teacher needs to do for the average students is to repeat the ideas and give more examples, while keeping the focus on the gifted. Instead, teachers strive to learn how to explain something to an average student, leaving the gifted students bored. The best thing is to explain to the good students, and go slower and be patient with average students.

Sport coaches understand this very well. They coach the students as if the student is a champion, knowing that of course most are not the greatest. Coaches focus on the great, while not ignoring the others. The focus is on excellence, not equality. Teachers, and not only coaches, should focus on excellence and not equality.

America was founded on the principle of maximum freedom and excellence to all. Most other countries in the world believe in equality of results for all, with redistribution of income to help achieve equality. Universities believe in student diversity, giving equal opportunity to all students, rather than striving to attract the very best students regardless of diversity requirements. America is now moving towards the European model of equality of results. This will result in a weaker economy, with people not fully capable of using their thinking to best deal with the challenges that lie ahead. America needs to reject the European model and restore the original model based upon the Constitution. Universities need to reject diversity requirements but to focus on excellence. Universities need to insure maximum freedom to faculty and not favor left-wing thinkers, and to examine sources of funding that restrict full academic freedom.

In summary, instead of trying to explain things to average students, teachers should think how they would explain it to smart students, and use the same explanations, just going slower, to the others. Let us give our admiration and praise to our gifted students and intellectually superior leaders.

Reading in high school
The article in the *U.S. News & World Report*, 2/28/2005, entitled "A new read on teen literacy" should be distributed to all school faculty and parents.

Here is an experience I had teaching a high school class. The students were assigned a chapter to read and take notes. I walked around the room asking individual students, "Tell me what you read."

"I do not know," some students said.

"You do not know how to read," I responded.

"Yes, we do know how to read!" they rejoined.

They must understand that reading for ideas is not reading for words as they did in the 3rd grade.

I asked them what are the topics covered, the supporting arguments, and if they agree with these arguments. I asked them if they could think of another example somewhere else where these same arguments would apply.

High school teachers must clarify that one of the goals of reading assignments is to teach the students how to read. In the 3rd grade, students learn how to read words. In high school, students must read and understand complex ideas. This is a skill that requires training and practice. Students must understand this, and actively work towards this goal.

Writing

Teachers need to explain to students how to use computers to write essays. The basic principle of rational thinking and idea development is to start from the beginning and do one step at a time. Let us apply this principle to writing. There are several steps. One is the development of the ideas and organization. The next step is to clearly communicate these ideas. The first step should be done with pen and paper, so that full attention is to the ideas. Many mistakenly start with writing on the computer. This is wrong, because part of your attention is devoted to dealing with the computer, such as pressing the correct keys. After writing the essay on paper, take a break, and then write the essay on the computer. At this time, automatic spell and grammar check must be turned off, so that your full attention is devoted to the clarity of the expression. Finally, as a separate check, do a spell and grammar check.

Professor Paul Krugman

Professor Paul Krugman clearly foretold in 2006 the current economic crisis. Although his writing was clear, eloquent, and insistent, he failed to get his message out. The question is why did he fail, and what lessons can we learn. This question is critically important for the future of our country America, especially now as we must make critical economic decisions.

Why did Krugman fail to educate the public about the critical economic issues they faced and the steps the government and public should have taken? Why was Krugman a bad teacher? Krugman is a professor at Princeton and Nobel Prize winner, which clearly indicates high intelligence, knowledge, and capability. Why did this gifted man fail the American public?

When I think about this, I think how I react to students.

There are certain things necessary to be a good educator, in addition to intelligence and knowledge. One is that the educator must give full attention to the students, be fully aware of their reactions and thoughts, and never ignore questions. Another necessary thing is the focus on basic principles. If the teacher sees that the principles are not clear, he must focus more carefully on the principles. We will show that Krugman failed both of these necessary things.

To try to understand Krugman's failure, we can analyze a specific event. In 8/2004, Tim Russert interviewed Krugman along with the Fox television commentator, Bill O'Reilly. The video of the interview and the transcript are available on line, so that they can be studied carefully.

The discussion centered on Krugman's new book. O'Reilly said that Krugman wrote that the Bush tax cuts would lead to a deeper recession. Krugman disagreed, saying he did not write this in the book; instead, he wrote that the tax cuts would lead to a "lousy job creation". O'Reilly said that this is the same as a recession, and started shouting and ranting at Krugman, who kept his cool simply denying it.

A news commentator has the objective and obligation to educate the public on his ideas, using rational logic based upon fundamental principles if this is how he feels. Once O'Reilly started shouting, he started using emotion rather than logic, contrary to his educational responsibilities. Currently, many Obama supporters use emotional anger defending their points. This is not rational thinking. We must insist that people discuss complex issues without aggressive emotions defending their positions.

This is how Professor Krugman should have responded. "Mr. O'Reilly, you said that my statement about lousy job creation is equivalent to saying that it would cause a recession. Is this correct?" O'Reilly would have to agree. Then the professor would make the point that lousy job creation is not the same as a recession. Krugman never made this point explicitly. This is a clear demonstration of Krugman's failure as an educator.

Giving attention and listening means understanding what they are thinking and building up from this. Krugman merely wrote columns twice weekly and analyzed issues, without connecting with us.

Educating the young generation not to be suicide killers

There is one way to change people, a way that has worked over the millennia of human history. This is education. If we can focus on educating the young generation not to be suicide killers, we will succeed in our efforts on the war on terror.

The first step we must all make is to talk about it. Every person who speaks or writes on this topic must always mention the education issue.

For example, we must remind British leaders that the shoe bomber was a product of a British school that taught suicide and murder. Just as one is not allowed based on free speech to yell "Fire!" in a crowded theater, one should not permit any educational institution to teach suicide and murder.

Whenever our leaders, make speeches, they must mention educational practices that teach suicide and murder.

As another example, Israel is now fighting the Hezbollah. When the media discusses the Hezbollah, they mention that Hezbollah also does important social work. The media must also add to these discussions the heinous educational teachings. We have to constantly repeat with clear examples how the young are taught to kill and die for nothing.

Five years after the United States began urging Saudi Arabia to eliminate extremist religious instruction from its educational system, a recent report by the international human rights group Freedom House found that Saudi textbooks still incite hatred against Christians, Jews and Muslims who do not adhere to the official Saudi brand of Islam.

Israel's *Intelligence and Terrorism Information Center* surveyed 25 new Palestinian textbooks published for the 2004-2005 school year. The books praise attacks against Israelis. Key facts of Israeli history are omitted. Israel is excluded from all maps. The Holocaust is omitted. No mention is given to the peace agreements concluded by Israel and the Palestinian Authority. The education epitomized by these books gives rise to new generations of students instilled with hatred against Israel, making peaceful coexistence between the two peoples highly difficult to achieve.

We are in the midst of a terrible world war, facing horrible possibilities. We must be courageous to fully analyze and debate our options. We are not doing this. Political pressures and pre-conceived ideas prevent us from fully open-minded discussions.

We do not discuss fully the nature of religion as the source of terror. We do not discuss education in Arab countries, which encourage suicide.

Every political statement must include details about Arab education for suicide and murder. We must constantly repeat details. Every scholarly work must include such details.

Walking down the halls on campus
Here is a little story that happened to me the other day that I wish to share with you. Walking down the halls on campus, I met a student who was in my math class last year.

"Hi! How are you?"

"I'm fine, Dr. Aranoff. Thank you very much."

"It is good to see you again!"

"It is good to see you also, Dr. Aranoff!"

"How are you doing this semester?"

"Very good. I am taking Statistics."

"How is it going?"

"Great. The professor is a very wonderful person."

"Very good. What are you learning in statistics?"

"Ah, ah... We are learning about variances."

"What are variances?" I asked, to encourage her to talk.

"Uh, uh… I don't know!" she exclaimed, looking at me with her wide-open eyes.

"It is important that you know the meanings of all the words that you learn in class," I responded, "Pay attention to the ideas and words and be sure you understand them."

She agreed, and continued walking up the stairs, looking as if she was deep in thought.

Isn't this what we are supposed to do here, to be engaged in deep thought?

Professors need to think deeply how to present the ideas to students and colleagues. Students need to think deeply to understand the ideas and relations with other ideas, to be able to focus on the highlights of the chapter or class, to know how to think logically based upon the principles they learned, and how to independently arrive at conclusions, checking for logical, empirical and historical validity. We need to understand emotions, for positive emotions generated by talking with people help memory and understanding, while strong emotions interfere with proper rational thinking.

When I look at students, I feel so happy, for I am looking at the future. They will need to mature to think independently, not to be swayed by a majority of others, to know what is meant by rational thinking and verification so that they will be able to deal with the serious problems they will confront. They need to know how to apply the tools and principles they learned to the unforeseen challenges they will face.

It is wonderful to be alive and to look ahead to the future!

Critical thinking
The *Wall Street Journal* said about Venezuela that coffee shortages predictably follow price controls. The question is that if it is predictable, then why do countries do it? If price controls do a great deal of harm, as Bruce Bartlett of *Forbes* wrote on 01/15/2010, why do leaders do such thoughtless actions? A country's leaders must think rationally about the problems, challenges, and goals of their country. We expect leading citizens, such as media people, pundits, and university professors to work hard to critically think about the issues facing their lives. Why do they not do it?

The answer to the question why do intelligent people fail to think critically is that they do not know how because their education did not stress critical thinking. This is a sad and dangerous reality. We can understand why the poor Venezuelan may not think clearly and so vote a dictator into power who destroys the economy. One Venezuelan told me that before Chavez there was plenty of food on the supermarket shelves, but not now. She voted for Chavez because he promised hope and change from the previous parties that were always fighting.

Critical thinking means that after reaching a conclusion or making a decision, the person must say he is wrong and then think why and what to do. Some newspapers print two editorials, one for an issue and the other against. This is not critical thinking, which is where the person making the statement must examine the contrary opinion. On television, we often hear debates between Democrats and Republicans. These debates are not critical thinking, which requires each Democrat to give sound reasons why the Republican position is valid, and vice versa.

The reality is that all knowledge is partial. Certainty does not exist. We can prove this mathematically. When a politician expresses complete confidence in a position, we must understand this as a confidence man, a con man, for he is lying.

This faulty thinking also infects, sadly, scientists, who often have complete, full, and unjustified confidence in their theories.

As a mathematics professor, I tell my students to check their answers themselves before looking for the answer in the back of the book. Our attitude is that we can depend upon authority, such as the teacher, professor, or the book, for the answers, when we must learn to depend upon ourselves with proper diffidence.

In summary, people who express full confidence in any position without giving serious consideration to the opposite viewpoint are irrational. Lawyers are irrational by this criterion, as they express opinions only supporting their side of the case. Statements made in commercials are irrational statements, for they never give serious weight to other opinions.

We can understand why politicians express one view and ignore the other view, as they want to win the election. Some politicians charge others with "flip-flopping" when they express a contrary view, and try to give the impression that flip-flopping is undesirable.

No Venezuelan leader can speak out saying that price controls will damage the economy. This means that Venezuelans are irrational people. Are we Americans also irrational? Can our leaders seriously discuss whether lowering taxes can increase government revenue? Can we say that asking banks to give mortgages to poor people at the same rate as people with good jobs will harm people needing housing? Can we say that the proposed two-state solution for Jews and Arabs in the Middle East will bring dangers and war but not peace, in addition to violating basic American principles against segregated housing based upon race?

We must educate high school and college students

in critical thinking. Media leaders must take the initiative in discussing what critical thinking means. Finally, voters must demand critical thinking from politicians.

Reliability and cost vs. benefit debate

When IBM was dominant (in the 1960s), software was completely reliable.

Microsoft discovered that one can make a lot of money by getting a product into the customer's hands soon. It announced delivery dates for products that did-not exist (vaporware). As soon as the product functioned at all, before the extensive and time consuming testing began, it delivered and made a lot of money. The rest of the world followed suit, because Microsoft is too strong to fight.

We have to fight back. We have to insist that vendors do proper quality tests by outside sources. When software is reviewed, we have to insist that the amount of time spent testing be included in the review. We also have to mention who did the testing - in-house or whatever. If we make this more public, people will buy from the vendor that tested for the longest time and so has the most reliable software.

Mathematics preparation

There is a lot of talk nowadays about the poor mathematics preparation our students have. As a mathematics professor, I will agree with this. Students coming out of high school do not understand that mathematics is a collection of principles that the students must master. Mathematics is critical for rational thinking. If Americans are unable to think rationally, our democracy will fail, and we will become a dictatorship like many other countries.

Here is an example. Students need to understand what insurance means. For the benefit of the reader, insurance is a system where a group of people pool money to cover large expenses that members of the group may occur. The annual payments to the insurance company must cover administrative costs and payments for expenses. The various insurance companies know from many decades of experience how to calculate the statistics to that the payments will indeed cover the costs. Now when the government, under President Obama's leadership, is attempting to require medical insurance companies to cover pre-existing conditions without increasing the payments, we all must understand that this is mathematical nonsense. Such statements are simply false. Anyone who makes such false statements, someone who otherwise is educated and knowledgeable, is someone who is out to deceive.

Educated people have the responsibility to educate others who do not know. Media pundits have the obligation to explain the mathematical nature of insurance, even if in so doing they will contradict the President of the United States, or the management of the broadcasting company where they work. If they are fired for speaking out, they should consider it as a brave act, similar to a soldier getting injured or killed fighting for our country.

When Congressman B. Frank insisted that banks give mortgages to poor people at the same rate as comfortable clients, he is talking mathematical nonsense. Unfortunately, no one pointed out the nonsense, with the result that the banks went along with this stupidity and then went broke. Because of national silence, Frank continues to be elected. We must be blunt, and speak out saying a politician who speaks mathematical nonsense is a liar and unfit to be elected.

I explain this to my university students. We must all do what we can.

When we deal with mathematics, there cannot be two sides. If the math is not valid, it is not valid. If this makes your entire position wrong, then your entire position is wrong.

When my students say wrong things, I do two things. First, I tell them the correct thing, pointing out their error. Second, I explain to them the faulty reasoning that led to the error. People tend to forget this second step.

The future of our country is at stake. Give me truth or give me death must be our motto. We must all speak the truth, even at the cost of becoming unemployed.

The mathematics of insurance is simple enough
for high school students to understand. High
school teachers must talk about it, in light of
current events in our nation's capital.

Question: Insurance companies know the
mathematical impossibility of covering
pre-existing without rate increases. Why are they
silent? Answer: By being silent, their stock goes
up. They are interested in short-term stock gains
at the expense of their companies. We have to
scream at the evil insurance companies that are
not fighting Obama!

5.   Israel

**Very few people correctly understand what
Israel is about, and what is going on.**

Many Americans are becoming homeless, due to
government policy mandating banks to issue
mortgages with terms more favorable than
customary and usual accounting procedures.
Unfortunately, we still deny the reality of this
forced government action, as well as frank talk
about solutions.

One solution for American Jews is to relocate to
Israel. Jews can become Israeli citizens upon
arrival, and eligible for housing, such as the
current housing in Jerusalem. Instead of
condemning Israel, Obama should help finance
this project to the extent that American benefit.

On the other hand, if Americans living in Israel
are harmed by the American policy of one-sided
condemnation and ignoring widespread Arab
anti-Semitism and illegal building, these
Americans can sue. The lawsuit would state that
Obama is not the legal president, as he has not
demonstrated his U.S. birth. It does not matter if
we think he was or was not born in the U.S. What
is important is that Israel goes on the offense, and
claim that Obama is harming Americans.

Building housing
Israel is a terrible country, building housing!
Especially at this critical time!

News item: Haiti government. has not built any housing for quake victims at this critical time. No condemnation!

If Israel did not build, left people in squalor, filth, and disease, the U.S. would then praise Israel.

The U.S. needs to be consistent. If government building is bad, such as the building by the Israeli government, the U.S. must stop supporting federal grants for homeless, and stop forcing banks to give cheap mortgages.

Instead of defending building, Israel must attack the U.S. housing policies which caused the recession.

Evidence is clear that the real aim of the Arabs is the destruction of Israel for religious and revanchist motives. Diplomacy is a tactic for buying time and camouflaging this motive.

A state faced with an aggressor but unwilling to confront him, whether because of fear, internal political constraints, or its own national interests, will use diplomacy to create the impression that something is being done, substituting words for deeds.

No to natural growth! This is exactly what Pharaoh, the ruler of ancient Egypt, said that Israelites must do. Moses complained to Pharaoh. We must learn from Moses, not to obey evil

decrees even for the sake of peace. We must
clarify this to Obama. Why do we refuse to
compare Obama to Pharaoh? Moses wasn't afraid.
Neither should we be afraid.

Tolerating rockets

We must stop taking about tolerating rockets. We
must do what American sing about in their
national anthem. Occupy Gaza like the US
occupied Nazi Germany, arrest all teachers of
hate, remove all books that teach hate. Tell the
Americans that they are racist for suggesting that
Israel talk to people who teach school children to
hate and kill.

Israel must demand money to repair damages
caused by rockets from Gaza. No money from the
U.S. to Gaza without equal money to Israel. The
monetary damages Israel suffered are equal to the
damages Gaza suffered. This must be kept
separate from the usual U.S. aid to Israel.

So much destruction!

Entering Lebanon in 1982, I was amazed.
Reading *Time Magazine*, I expected to find wide
areas of total destruction. Instead, a building here
with holes from shells, a building there. The
international media gave a false picture that Israel
did not refute. Israel must fight the world's media
to say the truth. CAMERA does a great job. I
want the Israeli government to do what
CAMERA does on a larger scale!

The two-state solution

The problem with Pakistan is the two-state solution there, one state for Indians, the other for Moslems. The world thinks peace will reign in the Middle East with a two-state solution, with Jews segregated in one ghetto-like state, and the Arabs in the other state. We must not make the Pakistani mistake again. We must do all we can to oppose the unsatisfactory idea of two states in the Middle East. We must try to solve the Arabs' problems within a Greater Israel.

Judaism has ideals of major significance to contemporary America.
The basic founding principle of Judaism is freedom. The primary festival is the "Freedom Holiday", Passover, celebrating the Exodus from Egypt. Egypt was a statist society. The government controlled allocation of resources and food, and dictated where people can live. See the Biblical story of Joseph who moved people across the country. The new Israelite society was free of strong government control, limited to judges and police. God tells us in the Bible that He has given us a choice between good and life, and evil and death; God then politely asks that we choose the good. Contrast this to Islam and Medieval Christianity, where the government kills those who reject the state religion.

The Hebrew Bible repeats many, many times the command not to forget the exodus from Egypt, from a statist society to a society of free people. We must constantly remember this, in the face of government trying to get more power and let people have less freedom.

During the festive meal on Passover, young people are encouraged to ask questions. Questioning is a hallmark of Judaism. Contrast this with the U.S. President Obama, who told students to pay attention. Questioning is an expression of one's freedom. Being told to pay attention is an example of government restrictions on freedom.

The American society was founded on the basis of these Jewish ideals. The American Revolution was similar to the Israelite revolution against ancient Egypt. The U.S. Constitution, expressing the ideal of limited government and specific enumerated powers, embodies the Jewish spirit of freedom.

The Jewish revolution took place 3 millennia ago. The American Revolution took place 3 centuries ago. The current counter-revolution towards big government started about 3 years ago. Jews have the obligation to speak out against current big government policies. Government control of manufacturing (such as automobiles) and medical services is contrary to both Jewish ideals of freedom and American ideals embodied in the Constitution.

In the Passover *Haggadah*, the wise son asks what are the rules and judgment relating to our society. Jews must discuss the Constitutional ideals of American society, pointing out that the approach of the Obama administration runs counter to American ideals. Jews must question the inherent logic underlying the medical insurance proposals. Jews must question the lack of candor in discussing examples of similar government insurance plans in other societies. Jews must stress rational thinking, which is the union of logical thinking based upon principles, along with empirical verification.

How can we best manage our affairs, to best function as a society and as a nation? There are two schools of thought. One school is that we need to follow leaders. The leader can be divinely inspired. This has been the case throughout most of history, from the ancient Egyptian pharaohs to the Catholic Pope. This is also the basis of modern religious thinking. People feel they can best live their lives following religious guidelines. In modern society, the leader can be an association of people, such as political and business leaders. The attitude is that leaders have more knowledge and experience. Children trust their parents, accepting the superior knowledge and experience of their parents. Likewise, many adults accept the leaders of society. The attitude is that it is best not to leave things to chance, to random choice, but to have control by leaders. This seems to be widespread in contemporary America. We are best off following leaders.

The other school of thought is that expressed by the American Revolution. Allowing people the freedom to choose as they wish, focusing on their individual benefits, is best for everyone. The complexity of economic life is too much for any wise group of leaders. The U.S. Constitution explicitly stated that the government must have limited powers. This school of thought says individual freedom will be better for all rather than following leaders.

Our government should be far away

In *The Fiddler on the Roof*, Tevye the milkman
says the Tsar is a great man, as long as he stays
far away. As a Jew, Tevye understood freedom.
We have to adopt Tevye's attitude, and demand
that our government stay far away.

Two sides
Secretary of State Colin Powell said the economic
pressure "does nothing to improve the security
situation." He blamed both sides for violence and
promised that when it subsided, President Bush
would play "a leadership role" in trying to
negotiate an agreement between Israel and the
Palestinians.

This is typical American nonsense. There are no
two sides. Only one side is to blame. The Arabs
are wanton murderers. They kill for no good
reason. Now we are supporting those murders.

The best thing the Americans can do is to stay
out. If we do not keep our dirty hands out of the

Middle East, we will get them chopped off.

We have other problems to worry about, like nuclear war and the nuclear capabilities of Iraq and Iran. We have to stop worrying about the Palestinians and Israel.

Talks with the Arabs
The American society is in deep trouble. Many Americans are losing their homes, and have no place to live. American Jews must seize this opportunity and move to Israel. The Israeli government is actively building housing for its people. The Obama administration is opposed, for it objects to government building housing. Jews must speak up and vote with their feet. Organized groups should move together into communities, where they can service each other - small businesses, medical and educational professionals, and such. Now is the time Jews must act. Jews must go up now to move to Israel.

Israel must learn from Honduras, who successfully dared to oppose the mighty U.S. The Obama insisted Honduras act contrary to the Honduras Supreme Court and take back the disposed president. Israel must make it clear that Israel will continue to build more housing for American Jews to leave the U.S. to come to Israel. Israel must stress the hate Arab kids learn in school, and demand that America address this hatred first. Palestinians do not build housing for Americans, for only Israel does.

Israel must say no talks with the Arabs. No talks with the Americans. No agreement that the Arabs can continue broadcasting hate. Say no no no, until Arabs stop teaching schoolchildren hate towards all Western ideas. America must understand the impossibility of peace when kids learn hate in school and in their churches.

The media reported, "Jewish leaders try to balance traditional deference to the administration with concerns over tensions." Deference is counterproductive to Jewish security. Never again to have deference to a hostile administration, as Jews unwisely did during Nazism. They will hear only if we shout loud. Say Obama is a racist for demanding separate but equal living spaces for people in Israel with different skin color, even if we think that the Jewish-Arab situation is different from the American situation, because we must be on the offense. Remind that Obama sanctioned Honduras, demanding they disobey their Supreme Court. No peace talks until Arabs stop teaching schoolchildren hate and Nazi literature.

A man who teaches young children to hate and kill is a wicked man. A country that requires by law that men teach youngsters to hate and kill is a wicked country. Nations that ignore teaching hate and murder are accomplices to this evil.

On *Yom Kippur*, the holiest day in the Jewish calendar, Jews read *Isaiah* 57:21, "There is no peace, says God, to the wicked." This verse is repeated in 48:22. When we read the prophets, we must not look at the material as predictions of the future but as aspirations of the Jewish people. Jews have believed for millennia that one cannot have peace with wicked people. Jews believe that it is impossible to have peace with the Palestinians for they teach kids to hate and kill. It is imperative that Jews get the message out to Israeli and world leaders not to have any form of negotiations, never to meet and talk, and, of course, never to make any concessions, until the hate teaching in Arab schools is properly addressed.

Israel must fight America!
Israel must fight the U.S., and learn from the Holocaust to fight. Never again will Jews accept big power dictates risking their lives! Here is how Israel can fight the mighty U.S.

1. Announce support of legal efforts to say Obama was not born in the U.S. Americans living in Israel can claim "standing" in court, due to the extreme danger Obama is placing Americans living in Israel in. It does not matter if the Israeli government really thinks this is true. The point is that they must say it, and give money to organizations fighting Obama.

2. Remind the world that the Jerusalem Arabs fought the Allies in WWII. Israel must occupy Arab lands as America occupied Germany, and use force to stop hate teaching in schools. Israel is silent on this issue. Silence means agreement. It

means Israel agrees that Arabs have international permission to teach hate.

3. Announce that Israel is planning an attack on Iran to destroy the Iranian economy, and will defend itself against any power, including the U.S., that tries to shoot down Israeli planes. It does not matter if Israel actually plans such an attack. The world must think Israel is ready to fight, and no form of sanctions will stop Israel.

Israel must take the initiative. Israel must speak out clearly against Obama's health care, saying this bad plan will destroy the U.S. economy and so hurt Israel. Since the U.S. is telling Israel what they must do in their most intimate lives, namely, where they can build homes, Israel has the right and obligation to tell Americans which policies they must support. Every Israeli speaking publicly must denounce the Obama health care plan. Instead of defending settlements, Israel must take the offensive! Many American citizens live in Israel, and can vote in American elections. There are very few voting Americans in Arab countries.

After World War II, the Allies occupied Germany, and used force against school teachers who taught Nazi ideas. Israel must occupy the various Arab regions under its control, and use force against school teachers who teach hate and murder. Peace talks must be on hold until the hatred is removed from educational and religious systems.

Some Jewish groups say quiet is the best answer. This did not work in the past. It cannot work, and it will not work. We must vigorously oppose Jewish organizations that suggest otherwise. For example, *J Street* says that various right-wing pundits "create a venomous attitude." It is *J Street* creating this bad attitude, not the pundits, who do not use such inflammatory words. If you disagree with someone, give logical reasons based upon basic principles, along with empirical confirmation, but do not use emotional words that hide the logic of your position.

J. Ben-Ami from *J Street* said regarding the Israel-Arab situation, "both sides must make painful compromises for peace." This is code for Israel that must make the compromises. They do not ask the Arabs for compromises. They do not mingle or interact with the Arabs. I taught high school science in an Arab school in Nazareth. We must reject groups like *J Street* that demand unilateral action from Israel.

The lesson of the Holocaust
Years ago, I spoke with Dr. Soloveitchik, brother of the famous rabbi. His wartime job was to tell the Allied planes the location of chemical plants. I asked him why he didn't lie saying the camps were chemical plants. His reply was that you just do not do such things. Today, Israel did not learn the lesson of the Holocaust. If the U.S. does not approve, you just don't do such things. Israel will not save Jewish lives by bombing Iran because the U.S. does not approve. When will they ever

learn?

Where can Jews live?

No one can tell Jews where they cannot live! We have to fight anyone who dares practice this anti-Semitic act of restricting Jewish living! In the 1930's Jews did not fight Nazi orders to avoid living in certain regions, in order to have peaceful relations. It did not help! The main thing we must fight for is freedom! "Give me freedom or give me death!" is the motto of Americans, not "Let us be friends and not have freedom!"

Let us not let America tell us that for the sake of peace Jews cannot live in certain areas, which the Arabs call the West Bank. Let us remind America that when the Governor of Alabama did not let black people have the freedom to go to certain schools, the American government got very angry and brought in guns forcing the Governor to let black students in the white school.

In 1974, I was very angry with the left-wing Israeli government that did not give freedom to Jews to live in the newly conquered territories, and participated in an all-night demonstration. Well, when the right-wing Begin government came into power, they denied the right of Jews to live in the Sinai. Later Begin's student, Sharon, used force to evict Jews from Gaza. They were all wrong in not insisting on freedom.

In 1951, my parents bought a home in Miami Beach, Florida, signing a deed that stated that they could not sell to black people. In those days, black people did not have the freedom to live where they choose. America has fought bitter struggles to let people have freedom. America never played it cool, saying that peace is more important.

Today also when America tells Jews not to build "settlements" in certain locations, let us tell America as clearly and explicitly that we will *NEVER* agree to such a terrible condition, even at the cost of economic sanctions by the world. Our freedom is paramount. First freedom, and then discussions about peace.

Yes, Jews must be allowed to live in the center of Arab towns and openly practice Judaism without fear. If trouble happens, the army must intervene, and arrest the bad people. Israel must stop being a country of two people that do not live together, and go to separate schools.

Many Israelis say that areas called "Palestine" by the Arabs are really areas that Jews have lived for millennia, and which God promised to Jews. These are areas where the various Hebrew prophets in the Bible prophesized peace. This is not the point. The point is that whatever the reason is, we must absolutely insist of freedom of living wherever before we can talk about peace.

The big mistake America is making in the world is the neglect of religious freedom, as mandated by U.S. law. The International Religious Freedom Act, over 10 years old, mandates that the promotion of religious freedom be a central element of U.S. foreign policy. Thomas F. Farr discussed this in *Foreign Affairs* March 2008. We must focus on freedom, including religious freedom, and then discuss what we can do to get the conflicts resolved.

Jews buying homes in Arab neighborhoods

An article on Jews buying homes in Arab sections of Jerusalem implied this was not a good thing. Why not? Don't we Americans believe that it is a good thing for white people to buy homes in black sections of the city, as President Clinton did in Harlem?

Democracy means that people can live where they choose.

Israel is not acting like a democracy, in not allowing Jews to live in various areas. The plans to evacuate Jews from Gaza were anti-democratic, similar to the apartheid in South Africa or Nazi German *Judenrien*.

We must not be surprised by anti-democratic actions by Jews in Israel against Jews. Evil to one's fellows is universal. We must pressure Israel to act like the democracy they profess to be. Municipal services must be the same for Israeli cities and towns in the West Bank. Schools should be integrated. People ought to be able to live anywhere, together. We must stop segregation in Israel, if we are ever to have peace in the Middle East.

6.   Religion

Ask questions

Jews ask questions. On Passover, children ask,
"Why is this night different?"

The Talmud, the set of books of the oral tradition,
begins with a question, "When do we read the
Shema?" The question is when can we begin the
morning prayers.

The Talmud says, "One who does not ask cannot
learn."

Other religions teach to obey and accept. The
American security worker does her job, and does
not ask questions. People hate Jews for the Jew
asking questions. Jews believe in freedom and
creativity.

Judaism's thirst for understanding

"How was your Passover Seder?" I asked my
daughter, who lives in Israel.

"We stayed up till past 1 AM," she replied. "The
purpose of the Seder is to teach the children."

Compare with a Seder at friends in New York:
We sang a few songs, drank wine, read parts of
the *Haggadah* in English, and ate matzo and the
meal. The children did not pay any attention to
the reading of the *Haggadah*.

Comparison of these two Seders shows that many

American Jews do not understand the profound message of Judaism. We are so overwhelmed by the messages from Christian leaders that we incorrectly view Judaism from a Christian viewpoint. The Pope's message is *obedience* to the ideals. Islam is based upon *submission* to God. Both Christianity and Islam stress the goal as individual salvation -- do as you are told, and then things will be better for you. This is akin to paganism, where one acts to please the gods so that the person or group will be better off.

The message of Judaism is so radically different that most of us misunderstand the message. (This may be a reason for the anti-Semitic hatred of Jews.) Belief in God is not central and basic in Judaism, as it the case with the other religions, for some Jewish authorities do not count belief in God as one of the commandments Jews are obligated to do (as, for example, the command to honor one's parents). Life after death is a formal belief and is downplayed. There is very little discussion of the Hereafter. Well, if neither belief in God nor a discussion of the Hereafter is the central message of Judaism, what then is the message?

The Talmud states, "It is better to do something good for its own sake rather than to receive a reward." This epitomizes the fundamental, critical difference between Judaism and other worldviews. Do the right thing because it is right, not to get a better place in Heaven, and not to make you feel good. This is the essential aspect of humanity as viewed by Judaism. This is not to be confused with altruism, but a full focus on the tasks.

The goal of scientific research should be our desire for knowledge, not for the applications that surely will follow. This attitude is a primary reason for the overwhelming numbers of great scientists who are Jewish.

Fighting wars is done for the purpose of defending ourselves, not for national prestige.

Jewish concept of the importance of saving one's life is different, and Jews need to explain the rationality and superiority of our way of thinking. Some members of the Islamic faith believe that one can murder people for the sake of religion. Quakers go to the other extreme, and will not fight to defend the country. Catholics translate the commandment "Do not murder" as "Thou shall not kill." A Jew is allowed to kill in self-defense.

Some feel saving another person's life is more important than saving one's own life. Jews have to tell the world that one's own life is paramount. Catholics believe that saving the life of an unborn baby is no less important than saving the life of the mother.

The very idea of fighting a war because we were attacked is not accepted. The U.S. gave many reasons for the invasion of Iraq, but did not say the reason was Iraq's shooting down our planes in the no-flight zone. When Arabs fire rockets into Israel and kill people, the world accuses Israel of overreacting, instead of understanding that Israel has the moral and legal obligation of self-defense.

The alternate approach to trying to achieve morality is to set up intermediate goals. Too many of us confuse these intermediate goals with the real goals. Too many of us focus on money or fame, or personal salvation via religion, and lose sight of the true goals we ought to pursue. Teachers, for example, give the impression that the goal is a good grade, rather than understanding, with the unfortunate result that students confuse the goal of good grades with the goal of understanding.

The Talmud states, "These are the things one gets rewarded both in this world and in the Hereafter ..." The items listed are things like daily prayer and doing kind deeds. The statement concludes saying that study is balanced against all the others. Study is the epitome of Judaism.

The core belief in education is why Jews are so successful in intellectual fields. There is nothing as wonderful as helping a young mind to think, learn, and understand. I am fulfilling the true essence of my humanity.

In these dangerous times, Jews must teach the world the important message of Judaism, if we are to survive. The current danger overrides the prohibition of teaching non-Jews the Torah. Jews must directly challenge the Pope's recent statement that obedience is paramount, instead stressing that understanding is paramount. Jews must directly challenge Islam teaching submission, where students learn to repeat back like a recording device. Jews must directly challenge, for example, Senator Hillary Clinton's statements that religion gives her comfort, and say that Judaism teaches to be focused on *goals*, not our comfort.

Jews must challenge our educational system demanding that understanding, not grades, be the goal. Tests that satisfy national goals must not be based upon rote memory. Jews must challenge U.S. foreign policy regarding Israel, saying that separation into equal states is not separate and equal; instead, Jews must demand America focus on the goal of Jews and Arabs working on joint businesses and ventures together, ignoring the intermediate goal of two states.

The presidential candidates speak confidently about their plans if elected. They are wrong in being confident, as no single human being has enough intellectual capability to properly understand the complexity of the issues. The president is chief executive, not chief. The correct approach is to support independent think tanks that have access to all relevant information. They would issue papers, and make them available on the Internet (after redaction). This would make the public more aware of the complexity of decision-making. Proper understanding of the conflicting goals of decisions, the different relevant historical analogies, and the various economic and political theories all are essential to good decision making. Here again the Jewish idea of understanding and complexity must be stressed. Jews must say that in-depth analysis is a basic Jewish concept.

A leader must be humble, not over-confident. Moses, our teacher, was "the most humble man in the world." Jews need to explain to others the need for humility.

A humble, honest person knows that *certainty does not exist*. In Hebraic law, if a court unanimously decides on a death sentence, the defendant is freed. The reason is that it is impossible to reach a unanimous death verdict, and so we suspect bribery. Modern scientific thought, as proven by K. Gödel -- an early 20th century mathematician from Princeton -- is that certainty does not exist. Jews have the obligation to stress that political candidates need to be humble and to acknowledge the complexities of issues. Jews must demand that people who discuss issues express doubt and admit they may be wrong, as this basic Jewish value has universal significance.

We must demand discussion of historical analogies with comments on the similarities and differences with the present. If a speaker fails to mention a historical analogy, we must demand that the person search for one, as there always must be analogies. For example, when we talk about leaving Iraq, we must discuss Vietnam, where we withdrew in spite of winning militarily. Millions died -- people who would be alive had we remained. The fall of Iran, and the possible future confrontation with Iran, was a consequence of our precipitous withdrawal from Vietnam. More recently, the withdrawal under fire from Fallujah, Iraq, during initial campaign approved by President George Bush four years ago may have resulted in the current civil war and the prolonging of our military effort. The discussion about Fallujah must include bad decisions made by governments during reelection campaigns. Any speaker on the subject of our current involvement in Iraq must discuss these historical questions. Jews must reiterate that such discussions are Jewish values.

When a speaker fails to discuss historical analogies, it means the speaker is trying to sell his ideas, rather than trying to understand the issues better. Judaism demands understanding, not salesmanship. The Torah says, "I have given you today life and good, and evil and death. Choose the good!" The Jewish value is to fully present the options, so that we can understand the choices.

We Jews must break our millennia-old silence. We must educate others about these basic Jewish values. These values are the focus on understanding, teaching, education, examining from all sides of issues, looking for analogies and parallels, honesty, humility, and explaining fully, including ideas with which we disagree.

The Pope on Creation

Pope Benedict XVI has waded into the evolution debate in the United States, saying the universe was made as an "intelligent project" and criticizing those who say its creation was without direction. He said some people, are fooled by the atheism that they carry inside of them, imagine a universe free of direction and order, as if at the mercy of chance.

This is not the Jewish idea. It is vital that we Jews stand up to the Pope and not leave his statements unchallenged.

The *Talmud* states in the end of the tractate *Sanhedrin* that there are questions one must not ask. One must not ask what was before (before Adam was created), what will be after (the hereafter), and so on. This is in accordance with the modern philosophy of logical positivism. The very successful theory of physics, quantum mechanics, which is the foundation of modern technology, is based upon the principle that there are limits on measurements. We can only measure so small, beyond which there is no meaning. In accordance with this, *Rosh Hashanah* is the anniversary of the first Sabbath, as time in Judaism can have meaning only when people are present to record the time. The first Six Days are therefore allegory. *If we take it literally, we are violating Jewish tradition.* If we use the story of the six days of creation to learn scientific theories, we are wrong.

Jewish custom is to keep religious thought
personal, and not discuss it with the world.
However, with modern communications, it is vital
that we correctly understand our heritage, and not
get confused by reading the pronouncements of
leaders of other religions.

Maimonides stated in his *Guide to the Perplexed*
that the belief that the universe always existed,
not that first God existed who then created the
universe, does not contradict basic Jewish beliefs.

There is no conflict between scientific theories of
the creation and Jewish belief. There is a serious
conflict in Catholicism, however, and this is the
issue raised with "intelligent design".

Evolution is a valid theory
A theory of science is based upon a mathematical
system, which is an arbitrary collection of
self-consistent statements, and which agrees to an
extent with observations and experiments.
Evolution is a valid theory. The mathematics is
consistent. Experiments and observations agree.
Creationism is not a valid theory. The logic is
inconsistent. Logical conclusions do not agree
with observation.

Israeli attitudes towards evolution
A recent survey of public opinion in Israel found
that 28% accept the scientific theory of evolution,
while 59% believe that man was created by God,

not by evolution. This is strange. The Talmud tells us "We must not to ask what happened before..." We are not allowed to inquire what happened before the creation of man. This leaves the possibility open for evolution.

The Hebrew Bible is clear. The beginning of chapter 2 of Genesis states that man was created from the dust of the ground, which is clearly evolution. This does not contradict chapter 1, which speaks about the creation of man meaning the creative thinking processes of people. Any religious Jew well versed in Jewish studies understands this and accepts rational scientific thinking, including evolution. This survey shows that many Israelis are primitive uneducated people. This survey shows the sad state of Israeli education.

Science and Religion – Seeking Common Ground
One says scientists should find ways of showing that faith and science can coexist. Why should they? Why, indeed, are scientists afraid to speak the truth - namely, that science denies the validity of all religious claims?

Our understanding of the world based upon science clearly conflicts with the idea of God from most religions. One religious scientist replied to me saying that there are many views that one can have on a subject. This is not correct if we are talking about knowledge, while it may be true for speculation and hypotheses for phenomena currently unexplained.

We are too glib in speaking about the how we can accept other opinions. For example, with the Israeli-Arab problem, there are not two sides, but one side – the Israeli side. The Arab "side" is evil propaganda that they teach young children to hate and kill, and so we must not dignify it by saying that their opinion is a valid opinion. Another example is the Democratic idea that the government can compel banks to give mortgages to people whom the banks know cannot repay the mortgages. This is a destructive idea, and we must not dignify it saying that there are two ideas, the Democratic idea and the Republican idea saying the government cannot compel banks to commit suicide.

The scientist who is dedicated to the pursuit of the truth must not waver in the face of powerful opposition, and should have the courage to speak out saying Christian and Muslim ideas of God are wrong.

Atheist prayer
The atheist and the Orthodox Jew can both pray. The Jew expresses his thoughts and feelings to God, which is infinite. This literally means without end. The atheist expresses his feelings to infinity. It is the same thing. Both are reciting beautiful poetry.

How God changes your brain
Review in amazon.com

D says: Are you being sarcastic? Or are you being serious? God is an idea that existed before science so we can't apply our scientific way of thinking? If you are arguing for any concept (god include) where we shouldn't use scientific method, logic and reason, then you are idiot. Using our minds (scientific method, logic and reason) is what got us the computer you are using to type your nonsense.

...

My reply:

First, please refrain from harsh words like saying I am an idiot, typing nonsense, or else we will get your post removed. Please apologize!

In science we begin by defining concepts, using observations. E.g., length is defined by the process of using a ruler. We cannot define god by using any observation or idea that exists. E.g., we cannot say God is a force when God created forces, and so we cannot define God using forces before forces were made. Therefore we cannot discuss God when we discuss science.

The scientific method that you refer to, using logic etc., starts somewhere. It starts with definitions and basic principles stated as mathematical statements. E.g., we assume $F=-GmM/r^2$, we define mass using $F=ma$, we define F using springs, we define a, r using rulers, and clocks. We use our logic, and predict tidal motion. Since we cannot write a basic principle including the God idea, God is not part of science.

If you believe in God, then accept the Hebrew Bible, which states, "No one can see Me and live," i.e., no one can understand God. Since we cannot understand God, it is not part of science.

Your job as a student is to understand what you are learning and to ask questions, but not to accept things just because your teacher or professor said so.

Okay, your homework, D, is to rewrite your post. Correctly define your terms according the rules of science discussed above. Apply rules of logic and arrive at conclusions. Let's see what you get.

Mark, you say, "The overwhelming consensus is that the majority of people, religious or nonreligious are kind and caring." I do not care for such inane comments! We here in America and in Israel are faced with extreme danger almost identical to the danger to the world the Nazi Germans posed. Then we did not take the danger seriously enough soon enough. The point is that Hitler clearly stated his plans in his book. Today Moslems clearly state their plans in their writings and teaching to children. We must fight and hit hard now in order to survive. We must also fight people like you, Mark, who speak about "kind and caring" people, when enough people are very unkind to scare us! Psychology 101: to achieve mental health we must accept reality.

"Your view on Islam is just the kind of
fear/hostility that we caution against…" This fear
is real. We must caution against belittling this
fear.

R says: Mark : I find myself in partial agreement
with both yourself and Sanford. Outside of
humanistic liberalism { or some compatible tosh}
there has never been a religion that claimed "the
majority of people are kind and caring" which
would be akin to cutting the hand that feeds them
{and easily falsified} . Even the etymological
roots of the word "religion" are derived from
restraint and, as Gandhi insisted, religion is
Morality in action. The division between Politics
/ideology and religion is largely artificial as
everything is rooted in religious worldviews - or
negations of religious worldviews - though
granted, extremist aberrations are sometimes
foisted on a people or nation by a small minority
that has managed to seize power.

Mt. Vesuvius

Plaster casts: Victims of the 79 A.D. eruption

Mt. Vesuvius erupted in the year 79, destroying Pompeii and other Roman cities. It happened on the same day that the Temple in Jerusalem was destroyed 9 years earlier. At the time, the coincidence of the dates prompted people to say this was God's punishment to Rome for destroying the Temple. In a 19th century excavation of Pompeii, an inscription was found saying "SODOM GOMOR[RAH]. This is discussed in *Biblical Archaeology Review*, July 2010. This is also available online.

We should tell Allah-fearing people if they continue to harm Jews and Israel, they can expect the wrath of Allah. Remember that Allah in Hebrew is the same word as God. We must talk to the Arabs using the words of God.

Cartoon of Mohammad

The reactions of our government to the cartoon of Mohammad are very wrong and harmful to our efforts fighting terror. The issue is not freedom of speech vs. religious sensitivity, as the conflict is portrayed. The issue is the evil support many Moslems give to suicide and murder.

Religious leaders must not speak in favor of suicide. Instead of defending the right of free speech, we must stress the cartoon's condemnation of suicide.

We must seriously charge the media and our leadership with the unacceptable silence on the issue of suicide indoctrination. This silence is akin to Chamberlain's acceptance of peace with Hitler. Britain paid dearly for the mistake of not speaking out against Hitler's writings. We too, will pay dearly in lives lost to suicide killers due to our mistake of not speaking out against suicide teachings.

Let us stop acting defensively about these riots. Let us stop saying that we understand their rage. Let us act offensively. Let us say that we are enraged at their acts of suicide, and will take all forms of action to stop this. Yesterday there was another suicide attack in which over a dozen people were killed. Let us remind the world that these suicide attacks are due to the religious training they receive. Let us remember that if we do not challenge their system, they will continue raising new generations of killers. Let us be brave and courageous, and fight this evil menace.

Neuron Bomb

The article "*Defusing the Neuron Bomb*" by C.F. Naff in the recent *Humanist* magazine upset me and scared me terribly. Naff coined the phrase "neuron bomb" to refer to religious ideology fusing into murderous belief.

America is faced by an enemy that wishes to destroy us, and we close our minds to the reality of this horror. We must not tolerate nonsense that some people like Naff say which only serve to further close our minds.

"Let us not make the mistake of singling out Islam. ... The vast majority of believers in every faith will never become neuron bombs. ... We have terrorist attacks from other people..."

These statements are scary. Okay, the vast majority of Moslems do not mean any harm. Let us say 99% of Moslems do not mean any harm. This is certainly a vast majority. This means that 1.5 million Moslems do mean us harm, and this is a large enough group to put our very existence in jeopardy. It is terrible that Naff wishes to calm us down using the phrase "vast majority".

The second nefarious error Naff makes is
mentioning believers of other faiths also are
neuron bombs, killing many people. This shows
an unacceptable ignorance of the Islam faith.
Read the Koran. Listen to the Islamic teachings in
their mosques and schools. The basic tenant of
Islam is that peace will reign on the world when
everyone unites in accepting Sharia law. A
Moslem will then kill people who reject this idea
in order to bring forth their messianic ideal and a
new world order with a single one-world
government. Yes, many Americans reject the
founding principles of the U.S. and are working
hard for a new world order and one-world
government; yes, these Americans will lie and
cheat to meet this goal; however, they will not kill
like the Moslems do.

What is tragic is the failure of people to
understand the Arabs, who are Moslems. The first
war America fought after our Revolution was a
war against the Moslems. Israel has been fighting
Moslem Arabs for its entire existence. However,
neither Israel nor America properly understands
the true dangerous nature of Islam.

A magazine like the *Humanist* and other
magazines that discuss religion and humanism
must discuss Islam, basing the discussions on
verses from the Koran. We need Arab speakers to
attend mosques to listen to sermons, and then
write about the content of these sermons. We
need people to read books Arab children read in

school. We need to talk to schoolteachers. We need to write what content is.

If we are to survive, we must be informed about the reality of the world. Naff wrote disinformation that is dangerous to all of us.

Church-state separation
This is an email I wrote to AU, Americans United for Separation of Church and State

There is another point that we must consider in addition to church-state separation. This is mosque-state separation. Islam is a very serious terrible danger. It is an internal danger to Americans. When public universities teach Islam and teach the importance of Sharia law and the need to overthrow America by force, then we must think about it. I would encourage the AU to go along.

Darfur
We are all concerned about the murder in Darfur. However, until we focus on the evil hatred of the Moslems, who hate as a matter of education and religion, there will never be peace. We fail to stress Moslem hatred. We are wasting our time, and losing lives!

Disaffected Muslim youth
CNN correspondent, Zain Verjee, commented about how the terrorists were "disaffected" Muslim youth with "grievances". This is false! They have no grievances! They are not killing

because of grievances! As long as we fail to understand the truth, we cannot succeed! The truth is their understanding of Islam. Will we wake up to face the horrible danger in front of us, or will we continue to view these serial murderers as people with grievances?

Hamas teaches children to hate

Forbes Magazine's June 17th online commentary, written by Professor Ian Lustick, was counterfactual. In his column, entitled "*Israel Could Benefit From Hamas*," Lustick redrew the nature of Israel's battle with Hamas from an existential one threatening the Jewish state to a religious battle against Islam. He said the terrorist Hamas regime is a peace-seeking organization which a jihadist Israel seeks to destroy.

In the late 30's we had to imagine a world without Nazis if we were to survive. We thought we could work together by giving them a little living room. We were terribly, horribly, wrong. We failed to realize and accept the reality that the Nazis wanted to destroy the world. Today we fail to realize and accept the reality that the Hamas and others want to destroy the world and make a new world order based upon Sharia law.

Professor Lustick discusses Muslims. Our job and responsibility as professors is education. When Lustick discusses Muslims, but fails to discuss schoolchildren learning to hate, kill, and to die, then Lustick is failing as a professor. We professors must focus on the evil education

Muslims learn in these primitive areas of the world, such as Gaza.

The Nazis also had an evil educational system. The guns and boots of the Allies forced the Germans to stop this evil teaching. Today, Nazi teaching is widespread in Arab countries like Gaza and Egypt. At the end of World War II we failed to finish the job. We worked on the German and Japanese educational systems, but not the Arab educational systems.

Lustick falsely claims that Muslim citizens of Israel, including Islamists, are uniformly law-abiding citizens who have not carried out terrorist attacks against Jewish citizens. In fact, hundreds of Israelis have been killed and thousands wounded by terrorist attacks carried out by Muslim citizens of Israel.

The Hamas web-based magazine for children, *Al-Fateh* has violent rhetoric. The website's violent rhetoric is not limited to Israel, however, at points threatening the United States:

"We are currently subjugated by the Jews, the Americans, and the British who occupy our holy land of Palestine, in Iraq, and in many Arab and Muslim states…it is [incumbent] upon us, the lion cubs of Arabism and Islam, to be prepared to fight those abject people and to liberate our country from occupation."

They preached many radical ideas, adherence to

the tenets of Islam, hatred towards Israel and the West, and the importance of committing acts of terrorism.

Dear Professor Lustick:

My point is that we professors must give the highest priority to education. We fail our fellow Americans by hiding in our universities. Professors should work with high schools, and spend a day as a guest teacher with the teacher observing. This is another point. Getting to your point, we need to focus on not permitting Hamas to teach schoolchildren hate. May I suggest you spend a few months in Gaza teaching? I spent a semester in Nazereth teaching physics, my field. Work to have some of your students teaching in Gaza.

When you write an article in *Forbes*, and fail to mention the education of the Arabs to hate, then your article is terrible. Hamas is a terror organization, and your article looks like treason to me, and so not protected free speech.

Both Bush and Obama are very wrong regarding Afghanistan. Until we force the schools not to teach hate, there will never be peace.

-Sanford

The Jewish God is not Allah
The Jewish God is a God of reason and rationality. People are created in the image of

God, and so are rational. Allah, the Moslem God, is a God of will and power. Rationality does not exist. One just does. Jews must demand that Arabs understand the need for rationality. Jews must fight the Arab educational system that stresses power and irrationality. We Jews will not make it if we do not directly confront the Arabs on their belief in an irrational God and irrational life.

Choice and control

We are not asked to eliminate our feelings, but to control them. Married men often meet beautiful women who try to lure them, as Rielle did to Sen. Edwards. The Hebrew Bible tells us, "I have given you a choice!" The essence of humanity is our ability to choose, not to act as our feelings seem to make us. Sir, if you are attracted to a married woman or to another man, control yourself and choose to do what is right!

Gays and the Bible

A newspaper article stated, "Garden State Equality, the leading advocate for gay marriage, criticized the lawmakers for renewing their efforts against gay marriage on Yom Kippur, the holiest day in the Jewish calendar." Criticism of gay marriage is one of the central themes of Yom Kippur. On that day we read in the Hebrew Bible God's order that a man not lie with another man like a woman, or partake in other sexual perversions, such as having sex with a man's daughter, with another man's wife, or with an animal. The text of the Hebrew Bible orders Jews not to be like other people, nor like the people currently living in the land they are going to. Jews have to learn on Yom Kippur not to be like other Americans and to avoid forbidden sexual acts.

Saying that some men have a powerful sexual desire for sex with another man justifies gay marriages is like saying that a strong desire for another man's beautiful wife justifies having an affair with her. God tells us in the Hebrew Bible to be a holy people to do the right thing, and to conquer our lust and avoid prohibited sexual encounters.

Yes, Yom Kippur is the proper day to speak out against making marriage between two men a legal marriage. Yes, it is fitting for rabbis to speak out on the pulpit for the idea of marriage between a man and a woman. Yes, it is proper for religious people who accept the Bible to work towards a constitutional amendment saying marriage is between a man and a woman.

Gays in the military
Discussing homosexuals in the military, some people wrote that this is different from obesity, which is a choice. Since homosexuality is not a choice, the military should not reject homosexuals.

This argument is illogical. If the military feels homosexuals will not help our military effort, then they can reject them. This has nothing to do with individual choice or our Constitutional rights. Americans do not have a right to serve in the military.

The question of the choice of homosexuality is different from the choice of one's sex. A man has no choice of becoming a woman, except by surgery. The homosexual chose that lifestyle. There is no scientific evidence saying that the homosexual has no choice.

Homosexuality is actually a religious question. The Hebrew Bible tells us that we have a choice to do good or evil, and asks us to do good. The Bible also tells us that it is a grave sin for a man to lie with another man like a woman. A homosexual man should control his desires for another man, just as any man must control his desires for someone else's wife. Christianity, on the other hand, teaches that everyone is sinful and needs God's forgiveness, and so there is nothing special about the sin of homosexuality.

American judges have no right to rule on religious questions. If the military does not want to enlist homosexuals because they feel it is against their religion, the courts cannot compel them to act otherwise.

A young man has the Constitutional right to be obese, lazy, and physically weak. I guess that the ruling on gay rights means that this obese young man has the right to join the military. It means that the F4 rejections are unconstitutional.

The judge is wrong. Americans do not have the right to join the military. The army is a duty, not a right. The army has the right to reject anyone it wishes. The army has the right to reject women as most women are physically weaker. The army has the right to reject mothers, as the Israeli army does.

I am very fearful about the future of America when judges can rule they way this judge ruled without loud protests from the media. We need to amend the Constitution to restrict the powers of judges to make changes contrary to the plain language of our Constitution. American citizens need to examine Article 5 of the Constitution, which gives the states the right to propose amendments without waiting for Congress.

Viewing other religions
Americans err in viewing other religions through the prism of Christianity. Many of us falsely assume that values and ideals that we deeply hold are shared by other religions. For example, we believe in tolerance and acceptance of others' beliefs, and incorrectly assume other religions are the same. We say that most people are like us, with the exception of a minority of extremists. When I studied Judaism for the rabbinate, the thing that surprised me the most was the fact that Judaism is so very different and so misunderstood by American Jews. The correct way to understand other people is to pay attention to the attitudes teachers teach young children in school. President Obama said in his message to students to pay

attention. I say to Americans to pay attention to the school lessons in Muslim regions, and do not pay much heed to official statements and pronouncements by leaders.

The prophet Jeremiah

The Bible reading in the synagogue for *Rosh Hashana* was *Jeremiah* 31:1-20. This is very beautiful and inspiring, describing the ingathering of exiles to Israel. These words have literally come true in our generation. However, we must not be mislead in understanding the Biblical prophets. These are not people who used magic to predict the future. Instead, the idea is that this represents Jewish thinking and longing throughout the millennia of Jewish existence. Jews have longed for centuries for a return to Zion and Jerusalem, for peace. Today the streets of Jerusalem are full of children shouting playing happily. Jews, both religious and secular, all over the world know this. It is important for Jews to remind themselves of this reality, and to constantly remind the world.

Education and peace

The *Rosh Hashana* High Holiday services were very inspiring and emotional for me. We read a prayer for peace. The prayer concluded with the hope that peace will come when the world will be full of knowledge. This is the key to peace that the American government does not get. The way to achieve peace in Afghanistan is by educating the people to Western ideals and knowledge, so that they can live in harmony and have the skills to be more productive. The key to achieving peace in the Middle East is not by restricting settlement building as Obama is preaching but by focusing on educating the Arabs to Western thought, culture, and technology. Arabs need to be educated that the teachings from the Koran for hate and murder are wrong, and Western ideas must replace the evil Koran teachings.

We must discuss education before we can talk peace.

7. Sex

Same sex marriage

There is a very important point on this topic that no one has discussed, in spite of the large attention this has gathered in the media and with our politicians.

The claim is not permitting gay marriages is discrimination, similar to the previous prohibitions against interracial marriages. This is simply false. The word "marriage" means, according to the dictionary, a union between a husband, who is a man, and a wife, who is a woman. This certainly was the meaning when these laws were enacted. There is no such thing as a marriage between two people of the same sex!

Some say that the word marriage includes marriage between two men. That may be today, and may have been true in some ancient societies; the majority of societies recognize marriage as only between a man and a woman.

Most historical writings clearly define marriage between a man and a woman. The Talmud, the basis of ancient Hebraic law and modern Judaism, is clear, quoting the Hebrew Bible, "If a man takes [marries] a woman..."

Wikipedia. http://en.wikipedia.org/wiki/Marriage, has some quotes:
"Edvard Westermarck defined marriage in his book *The History of Human Marriage* (1921) as '

a more or less durable connection between male and female lasting beyond the mere act of propagation till after the birth of the offspring.'"

"The anthropological handbook *Notes and Queries* (1951) defined marriage as 'a union of a man and a woman such that children of the woman are recognized as legitimate by both parents.'"

There is a confusing point about the definition of marriage. Some say that once a legislative body creates a law recognizing marriage between two men as identical to marriage between a man and a woman, the definition of the word marriage now includes marriage between two men. However, legislation can only add to the meaning of a word, but not change it. Many words in the dictionary have several meanings. The legislation cannot delete the previous meanings.

For example, New Jersey legalizes gay marriage. This means that in New Jersey marriage between two men is marriage according to the word marriage. (Let us ignore for now the issue that the U.S. government does not agree to this definition.) Today in New Jersey when one reads an article or book written prior to the legislation, marriage means only between a man and a woman. The legislation cannot change the meaning of words prior to the legislation.

This is clarified by Webster's definition of marriage. Miriam Webster,

http://www.merriam-webster.com/dictionary/marr
iage,
states: 1 a (1): the state of being united to a person
of the opposite sex as husband or wife in a
consensual and contractual relationship
recognized by law (2): the state of being united to
a person of the same sex in a relationship like that
of a traditional marriage.

Webster added a new definition to marriage, but
did not remove the original definition. To repeat,
one definition of marriage is marriage between a
man and a woman (or women). This has been the
definition of marriage throughout history, with
some small exceptions.

In this context, let us remember the quote of
Abraham Lincoln, "If you call a tail a leg, how
many legs has a dog? Five? No, calling a tail a leg
don't make it a leg." Calling union between two
men marriage does not make it marriage.

Many laws use the words like "civil unions" and
such to avoid confusion between different
possible definitions of marriage. These unions can
be two people of the same sex, or a man and a
woman over the age of 62. However, these laws
miss the point.

Sexuality is an integral part of our humanity
The point that we must never forget that sexuality
is an integral part of our humanity. We are not
just people. We are men and women. To deny this
is to deny reality and to distort human

relationships.

This began with an assault on the language. Most languages have clear gender distinctions. We are trying to get rid of this in English. For example, we use the word "chairperson". We are trying to say that it does not make any difference if the chairperson is a man or a woman. This is not true. *Saying this is denying the humanity of the chairperson.* It is like calling the chairperson "it", instead of "he" or "she". It is not good! E.g., "The student came home from school, and it started studying." (Or he/she started studying).

Actually, the word "man" refers to a person of either sex, for man is human with the "hu" removed. If we wish to discuss males, we cannot correctly use the word man.

The reality of human sexuality is beautiful and mysterious, and we must not ignore our feelings and our selves!

Another example of the evil of ignoring human sexuality is the way these subjects are taught in our schools. Children learn about diseases that can be caused by sex (STD's). However, they are not taught the positive beauty and wonder of sex. No one tells them that when they become independent adults and marry they will have a lifetime of great sex. Because of this, they tend to view their feelings as something they have to give into right now, and not discuss this with their parents and teachers. We have to change the approach we now have in our schools in how human sexuality is taught. This not only will help the children become happier adults, but will also help keep them healthy, and not sick with STD's.

The logic is that if we totally ignore our true sexuality in all of our discussions, then indeed the gay marriage movement has validity. The issue is not gay marriages, but our approach to our sexuality. Enthusiasm for acceptance of sexual relations between two men must not be allowed to hide the importance and reality of sexuality between the sexes, which insistence on hiding the original meaning of marriage does.

Sexuality in the Hebrew Bible

This article discusses various verses in the Hebrew Bible relating to sex. The translations from Hebrew are my own free translations.

Many people fail to appreciate the primacy of sex, and do not really want it. I hope that you, my dear reader, will think about these, and to focus your lives and attention on sex, in order to be happier people.

Sex is the most important, most beautiful activity that exists. Ask me what single thing do I wish more than anything else, and I will answer: a normal sex life. If we wish to achieve anything in life, we must first articulate our desires. We must clearly express our goals if we want to achieve them. I have been thinking that the failure of marriages today may partly be due to lack of focus on sex. Yes, people have great sex. Yes, people love each other, are friends, confide in each other, express intimate feelings. People, however, do not discuss sex as a goal. Is it because we are religious? Well, Judaism encourages loving sex in marriage.

Is it right to say you want sex as a primary goal? Or shall we strive for other things, and enjoy sex if it happens? The latter is what one is probably taught in school. My point here is for the sake of human happiness we have to focus on sex as a goal to achieve.

The next question I asked myself is why? Why do we so earnestly desire sex? Well, sex is a unique human activity for several reasons:

1. It is the only human activity that requires two people to do it together. There are many activities that we do together, but every other activity can also be done by ourselves. It is better to play in a group, but a solo player is also possible.

2. It is the only human activity that fully unifies the physical and mental. Eating is primarily physical, although we can color food. Mathematics is primarily a mental process, although we can have colorful designs to give us sensuous pleasure. Sex requires that we focus on the other person, on her thoughts and feelings, as well as her beautiful body.

3. Sex is the most enjoyable activity that a person

can possibly do. Every sense is fully stimulated to
the extreme. When my naked wife walks into the
bedroom, it is the very most beautiful sight I have
ever seen in my entire life. When we touch, it is
the most pleasant feeling ever felt. When she
talks, her voice is the most pleasant sound I have
ever heard. When I smell her body, clean from a
bath without any perfume, it is the most beautiful
smell I have ever smelled. Moreover, of course,
her food, made for me with her love, is the tastiest
food ever eaten.

Let us examine how sex is mentioned in the
Bible, starting with Genesis. The moral lessons
are hidden there, hidden by redundant phrases and
the proper choice of words. Joseph was called
"the decoder of the secret things."

Sex begins with God saying, "It is not good for
man to be alone. I will create a helpmate."
Strange verse. God created the entire universe, but
forgot something. Made a mistake? No. God did
not make any mistakes. It is not that God
suddenly realized it is not good for man to be
alone, but that man realizes this at some stage in
life, and begins looking for a wife.

"Adam had sex with Eve his wife . . ." The phrase
"his wife" is redundant. There was only one
woman named Eve in the world at the time! This
phrase is to emphasize that man has sex with his
wife only, not with any female, as do the animals.

The word "had sex" in this verse in Hebrew is the

verb "know." This is a very strange verse. It is saying that Adam knew his wife, and then she became pregnant, etc. Before this, he did not know her. What does "knowing" have to do with her becoming pregnant? The Torah is telling us a point - a lesson. In order for the sex to be properly done, man has to think about the woman. He has to be aware of her feelings, her presence. Sex begins in the mind. If a woman says that a man wants her only for her body, she does not understand sex, for sex requires both the body and thoughts.

Let us continue with the book of Genesis. Abraham was the first of the three patriarchs. He went to Egypt with his wife Sarah. An entire discussion of her great beauty appears. How the king desired her because of her beauty, etc. So what if the king (Pharaoh) lusted after Sarah? The story of Sarah's beauty has nothing to do with Pharaoh trying to rape her. It has to do with us. Sarah represents the ideal Jewish woman. Such a woman is very beautiful. Why? Because she is serious about her physical condition. This all Jewish girls know very well. When the women donated their mirrors to the holy sanctuary, Moses at first refused to accept them, until God told him the women used these mirrors to make themselves pretty, and so they were sacred objects!

Isaac, Abraham's son, was the next generation. The story how he met his wife is so beautiful. Abraham's worker going abroad, giving presents to Rivka. This is the nature of courtship, today as

well as three thousand years ago. One gives
presents to the girl. This makes her feel good,
ready for sex. I stress the sex, as we must never
forget the primary goal of our actions. Therefore,
presents, gifts, jewelry and candy, these are all
parts of having sex.

"Isaac married Rivka and loved her." Isn't this
backwards? First one falls in love, then get
married! Isn't this the theme of most romantic
stories? Let us not say in those days they married
first, before falling in love. Remember, the Bible
was written in code, and there is a point, a
message to this. As a child, I asked my parents
this question, but never got an answer. Now I
know the answer.

Let us look at the entire verse. "Isaac had sex with
Rivka, he married her, and he loved her." The
word sex is, in Hebrew, "he brought her into his
house." Bringing in, in Hebrew is sex. The act of
sex changes a person, changes one's hormones,
creates love. Someone said that many people have
sex without falling in love. My reply is that if we
have sex properly, by first thinking (as Adam
did), then noticing the beauty of the girl, then
doing all the proper things, love will develop.
There is no doubt of this in my mind. First sex,
then bonding and love. This is the reality.

What is wrong with today's society? The failure to
focus on sex. If a couple has good sex, they
should be very happy with their accomplishments,
and make a serious determined effort to continue

to have good sex as one of life's goals. This decision, this determination, is love. We need to appreciate the good that we have.

"Isaac had sex with Rivka. The king looked out the window and saw them. The king summoned Isaac and said that Rivka was his wife, not his sister . . . " Strange story. Having sex right in front of the king's window! Wow! What a hot man Isaac was! Puts Don Juan to shame!

The interesting thing is the verb in Hebrew used for "having sex." It is playing. Isaac was playing with Rivka. This is the next essential aspect of sex. You must play and have fun. If you are not playing together, it is not sex. Today we call it "fooling around." This is good.

When Isaac became old, he became blind. Rivka said, "I despise my life because of these girls my son Esau married." She did not despise her own life because of what her son did! Since Isaac was blind, he could not see Rivka, and so could not get sexually stimulated. Once she had no sex, she does not want to live any more. This again stresses the centrality of sex. It is the main and primary focus of all of our lives and actions! This is the message of "I despise my life." We must not make the error of thinking that a family, children, friends, and all such good things are more important than sex! Again, it is necessary to focus and articulate our goals in order to achieve them.

Let us go to the next generation, Jacob. He worked for seven years for his wife Rachel. When Jacob first saw Rachel, "he kissed her and cried." Kissing is an essential part of sex. Kissing, touching, embracing. We cannot have sex without first kissing. We do not have to kiss just the moment before sex. We can kiss seven years before. It is all part of sex. What we are saying here is it is good to kiss on the first date. This act of closeness expresses our mutual feelings.

After the seven years, he said to Laban, "Give me my wife so that I can have sex with her." The great Biblical commentator Rashi asks, "The most common man does not use such language. How can the saintly Jacob talk like this?" Rashi then goes on to give some type of answer. I like Rashi's question, not the answer. Jacob came to the point. Sex is the central issue. It is essential to talk about sex, and not be falsely modest. Only by so talking can we become happy and well adjusted.

Let us go to the next generation. Jacob has 12 sons and one daughter Dena. One day she goes to the next town, meets a boy named Schechem the son of Donkey (Hamor in Hebrew). This is in the hilly section north of Jerusalem. Donkey was the king of the district. Schechem "spoke to her heart," had sex with her, and fell in love with her. He proposed marriage to Jacob. Jacob's sons tricked Schechem and killed him and his family. Jacob asked them why. Their response, "Shall our daughter be treated like a prostitute?"

First, why the great concern with prostitution? The senior brother, the boss, Judah visited a prostitute. King David was born from this relationship.

Strange story. Many religious schools simply skip this story. Many translations of the Bible simply do not translate this part. Now I understand what this is all about, and what the true message is.

We can all agree that cold-blooded murder is wicked. Indeed, later Jacob condemned his sons for the murders. The point is that just as we can all agree that their actions were very wrong, so also was their comment about Dena being like a prostitute very wrong. We are to understand this correctly.

Remember the movie *Pretty Woman*? A rich man takes a pretty prostitute into his house, tells her he will give her all the money she wants, but she has to stay with him, and not have sex with other men. The movie goes on making fun of her as a prostitute. They got it all wrong!

What is a prostitute? Why do we condemn prostitutes? Why do we say when we do something we do not like we are prostituting ourselves? We got it all wrong today, because we fail to fully appreciate the Biblical story of Dena!

First, there is nothing wrong for being paid for sex. Indeed, this is the very basis of marriage. A man pays a woman to have sex with him, on a long-term basis. The Talmud discusses this, "There are three ways a woman becomes married. One is giving her money."

The moment Pretty Woman agreed to stay at the man's house she became his wife and ceased to be a prostitute!

What then is the evil of prostitution? Answer: a prostitute is one who constantly changes partners! This is the evil. Not the money for sex problem. It is good to take money for good actions. We work for a living. Are we prostitutes, taking money for good deeds? No!

Remember Jackie Kennedy, one of the most beautiful women whoever lived, wife of President Kennedy? After he died, she married Onassis. People said she married him just for his money, as he was the richest man in the world. People said she was a prostitute, and to be despised. Wrong! She knew that she could make him very happy. She stayed at his side as long as he was alive. By the way, she got a lot of money. Wonderful.

This is the message of the Dena story. Never, ever, think that sex with someone who loves you is prostitution!

There is another point: "And he spoke to her heart." This is another essential aspect to sex. It is not enough to be beautiful, to give gifts, to kiss. We must talk and express our feelings. We must tell each other what we want from each other. We must express our desires in clear words. Just because people are in love does not mean that they "understand" each other. We tell the other person that we want to kiss, to be kissed, and to have sex together.

Jacob's son Joseph. Joseph was very handsome. "Girls would climb walls to see him." What a beautiful verse. I, too, was very handsome. In high school, the girls would yell out to me, "Sanford, I love you!" Well, Joe got this job as a manager in Potepar's house. Mrs. Potepar daily said to Joseph, "Sleep with me!" Joseph refused, saying that his boss gave him control over everything in the house except her, as she was his wife. This stresses the theme that a woman belongs to one man and no one else.

In summary, we see that the verses in the first book of the Bible exactly mirror the sex life of people, in the sequence of which it actually occurs. The first phase is "no good" feeling of being alone. The next is beauty. The girl making herself beautiful, and the boy noticing the pretty girls. The next is meeting each other, and the boy giving gifts to the girl. Next is playing and having fun. Next is close physical contact, kissing. Next is talking about your feelings, emotions, and goals. Finally having sex, realizing that sex is the greatest gift of God to man, the most wonderful experience anyone anywhere can have, the most beautiful . . .

Men and women are different.
This reality is misunderstood. Too many modern
Americans think men and women are just people,
with different genitalia. This lack of proper
understand causes us to be very unhappy.

Women need understanding, attention, and
appreciation of their feelings. This desire for
understanding of feelings is sometimes so strong
that they tend to overlook proper rational
thinking. I was talking to two young women. One
was saying how very busy she was as a mother of
young children. I tried of offer a suggestion. The
other woman said that she does not want to hear a
suggestion, as she just wants to express her
feelings.

Men are different. Let us imagine what the bee says to the flower, and what the flower says to the bee.

The bee is flying around, and sees a flower.

"Looks like a pretty flower! Let's check it out!"

"Wow! It smells good! Oh, this nectar tastes so good! Oh, how wonderful! Oh, oh, zzzzz, how great!"

"Was that ever wonderful!"

What does the flower say to the bee?

"Hey, big boy, I'm here whenever you want. I have nice honey. You are welcome to come anytime! I'm open for you!"

The bee needs permission from the flower. The
bee needs the signals, initially visual, for
permission. The man needs permission. A man is
attracted to nudity, which is a powerful signal for
permission. Of course, a man also needs
understanding, but permission is the dominant
need.

The sergeant tells his men during target practice,
"Ready, aim, fire!" The Israeli sergeant says,
"Ready, aim, at your free time, a fire!" No one
commands a soldier to fire his weapon, but
instead gives him permission. This shows the
critical importance to the man for permission.

Here are some examples of sad things that
happened to people. Mrs. Clinton decided to sleep
in a separate bedroom, as the couple had different
schedules. Mr. Clinton knew he had no
permission to enter his wife's bedroom. He later
on noticed that some of the young girls in the
office looked at him with great respect and
interest in whatever he had to say. The end was
that he said, "I did not have sex with that
woman!" Society blamed Mr. Clinton, for not
controlling himself. Actually, how much
self-control does a person have? Personally, I
blame Mrs. Clinton for the failure to understand
that a woman must never give the man the
impression that he does not have permission.

After the Woods' divorce, Mr. Woods said that he
made terrible mistakes. He did not say, nor did he
understand, what the mistakes were. His mistake

was not understanding his need for his wife's permission to be near her always. Mrs. Woods was crying like a little girl, saying tearfully she did not expect this to happen. She should have expected it to happen, for she should have understood a man's needs! She should have gone with him in his travels. After a hard day golfing, he comes home, showers, and then sits down and talks with his beautiful wife, one of the most beautiful women around, and then thinks about her. When people talk directly and make eye contact, there are emotions. He would simply have no time to think about anyone else.

I tell my mathematics students the need for emotions for them to better understand and remember the material. The way to get emotional about mathematics is to talk to each other making eye contact. Using machines, such as phones or email, does not create emotions.

Mrs. Woods needed to be physically next to Mr. Woods much more often. This was their tragic mistake, that will cause them to be unhappy for years to come.

There are there major reasons for sex. One is procreation. The second is pleasure. Sex is one of the greatest pleasures a person can experience. This pleasure reason is so important that Jewish law commands a man to have regular sex with his wife. The Hebrew Bible says, (Ex 21:10) that a man must not reduce his wife's food, clothing, or attention.

There is a third major reason for sex, which sadly not many are aware of. A man is like a bee in the sense that a man's mind is always wandering, exploring, looking for things. The woman needs to understand this and keep the man's mind busy with her so that he would simply not think of other women.

Brilliant, successful Mr. Spitzer surprised everyone when he spent so much money on a recent college graduate. I blame Mrs. Spitzer for probably saying to her husband that she was tired and just wanted to go to sleep. (Actually, I do not know, of course). Mr. Spitzer understood that he had no permission that evening. He started thinking about what he heard the other day in the office about these young women...

I know a young man who had a very cheerful, friendly disposition, but whose wife was tough, boastful, a no-nonsense person. He showed me his large stack of *Playboy* magazines. I wondered why a married man would read *Playboy*. Maybe because his wife felt there was no need for nudity. If so, he knew he had no permission to see his wife's nude body. This meant he was frustrated. He died as a young man from a terrible illness. I wonder if the lack of understanding the differences between men and woman caused his untimely demise. It makes me think that a healthy normal sex life is important to health and longevity.

Men and women are different, and we must understand these differences. As the French say, "Vive la différance!"

If a man takes a woman...

We can see another major misunderstanding of men and women in contemporary society in this verse in the Hebrew Bible, Deut. 22:13: "If a man takes a woman…" Note that the man takes a woman for a wife, not the woman takes a man for a husband. In Orthodox Judaism, the marriage ceremony consists of the man giving a ring to the woman. Today's liberal Judaism modifies this with the woman also giving a ring to the man. The idea is that two equal people are marrying each other. This sounds beautiful, but unfortunately does not jive with the reality of the sexual differences between men and women. The man aggressively takes the woman, with the woman giving permission. The man asks the woman out for a date. The man drives to the woman's home, where she invited him. In order for mutual satisfying sex to take place between a married couple, the man must take the attitude of "taking", that is, taking the initiative. This is a mental attitude is very important.

It is interesting to read the rest of the above verse. "If a man takes a woman, comes to her, and hates her…" Why should he hate her after first deciding to take her? We must understand that sex involves two people, each doing their part. The man did his part, choosing the woman and taking her. She has to do her part to accept him. If she does not, that

is, she does not give him permission to come to
her, then his feelings towards her will dissipate.
The woman must realize that her responsibility is
not only deciding to accept the man, but to
continue making him feel that she accepts him
and gives him permission to come to her.

8. The Big Lie of God's Existence

Religions, belief in God, prayer, rituals, all these things are beautiful. Especially when the entire family participates in the religion together, and we pray together with our friends. Religion gives us meaning to life and to help us cope with the mysteries of the universe. Religion makes us and our children to be better citizens, to be more ethical and moral people.

Wonderful, very popular, beautiful, and false and evil.

Once upon visiting Europe I asked a native for directions. I received a clear, precise, and incorrect response. This is my attitude towards religion: clear, precise, and wrong.

I. God cannot possibly exist

God's definition. First, it is impossible to define God. Moses Maimonides (1135-1204) expounded on this idea. See *"The Guide for the Perplexed"*, by Moses Maimonides, translated by M. Friedländer (Dover, New York, 1956). Modern man forgets this. If we cannot define what the word "God" means, how can we speak about our belief in God? How can we discuss God's existence if we cannot even define the word?

God existed before the creation of the universe. Consequently, we cannot use any physical concepts in our definition of God. Before the creation of the universe, God was unique, and so could not be defined. The very uniqueness of God, as expressed in the Shema, "Hear Oh Israel God Our God is One," precludes any definition of God. To repeat: Because God is unique, he cannot be defined!

Another way of saying this: The universe is everything that exists. If God created the universe, then God created God, which is logically false.

God's omniscience. A basic characteristic of God is His omniscience: "Having total knowledge; knowing everything," to quote the Heritage dictionary. These ideas are simply impossible.

James Clerk Maxwell alluded to the problem with God's omniscience a century ago in his major work in theoretical physics, in the study of thermodynamics. He coined the phrase, "Maxwell Demon." A Maxwell Demon is an intelligence who sits at the mouth of a balloon that is releasing its air and contracting. This Demon knows the position and velocity of each molecule. This motion is random. Why cannot the Demon control things so that the balloon would automatically expand? Yet this never happens. Why does a car tire go flat when a nail punctures it? Why does not the tire just fill with air by itself, since the motion of air molecules is random? Air does not go out of the tire due to the "pressure" of the air in the tire, but due to random motions of the molecules. Maxwell proved that physics would be very different if a Maxwell Demon can exist.

Therefore, it is impossible for God to have an intelligent knowledge of the motion of the molecules of air in the tire. This is proof of the impossibility of God's omniscience.

Liquid Helium. Helium, one of the lightest gases, remains a liquid down to absolute zero, unless high pressure is applied. At 2.17 Kelvins, normal pressure, the liquid stops boiling, and becomes a superfluid. Why? The reason is quantum mechanics. When helium solidifies, each atom occupies a location known within an accuracy of the lattice site. This knowledge causes an uncertainty in energy, as given by the Heisenberg Uncertainty Principle. For most pressures, this energy is larger than the weak binding energy, and so helium remains a liquid. In other words, not even God can know the positions of each atom. Hold up a vial of superfluid liquid helium. The fact that you see a clear liquid is proof to the uncertainty of the positions and velocities of the atoms.

Rate of travel of information. Information travels at a finite speed. When we look at the sun, we see what was there eight minutes ago. A space ship near Jupiter sends a radio message to us that takes an hour to arrive. We therefore know only what happened an hour ago. This concept was originally formulated by Albert Einstein in 1905 in his Special Theory of Relativity, and has been verified by countless experiments since. To say that God knows what is happening now both on earth and on Jupiter at the same time is simply impossible. Another way of saying this is this: For information to travel faster than light is equivalent to information going from the present to the past and influencing the past, which, of course, is logically impossible. These ideas are well known, and so it is very surprising to me why they are not stated more clearly.

Kurt Gödel. In 1931 the mathematician Kurt Gödel published the *Incompleteness Theorem.* See http://www.miskatonic.org/godel.htmlhttp://www.miskatonic.org/godel.html

This proof states that within any rigidly logical mathematical system there are propositions (or questions) that cannot be proved or disproved on the basis of the axioms within that system. It is therefore impossible for any logical system to be complete. For example, if we have a mathematical system of arithmetic, which consists of axioms ($a*b = b*a,$ etc.), there will always be a statement that is true, but cannot be proven on the basis of the axioms. If we include this statement as an axiom, we will find another true statement. There is more to be known about any complex system than can be deduced from basic principles.

We can use computers to calculate the future. E.g., on the basis of our observations, we can calculate the position of the moon next month. Some calculations are very hard, and take a long time, even on powerful computers. There are events whose calculation is so hard that if the entire universe were one big computer, the time it would take would be greater or equal to the time it takes for the event to actually happen. A simpler way of stating this is this: Some things cannot, in principle, be calculated. Not even God can know what will happen.

II. God is not needed

Imagine a scientist standing by the shores of the Red Sea as it was split, allowing the Israelites to escape the Egyptians in the Bible. Would he or she say, "Wow! Only God could split the sea like this!" No, of course not. She would say, "This is an amazing phenomenon. I'll have to study it more to understand it." God is not needed to explain the universe.

Science does not explain everything, nor does it try to, as discussed above. Instead, science tries to explain as much as it can. The unexplained is left for the next generation of scientists to probe.

Morality. We do not need God as a basis of morality. We can be very moral and ethical based upon basic principles of the value of mutual cooperation. This has been demonstrated by many psychological experiments. Furthermore, religion is fundamentally immoral, as it teaches actions that are not in the best interests of people. Since religion is false, teaching religion is immoral, as it is immoral to teach lies.

There are those who say that without belief in God morality does not make sense and life is meaningless. That claim is false, as is pointed out by the *Britannica*, for even if there is no purpose to life there are purposes in life - things people care about and want to do - that can remain perfectly intact even in a Godless world.

Religion causes wars and hatred. Anti-Semitism is essentially a result of religion. Look at the evil wars in the name of Islam. Look at the Irish terrorists and Muslim terrorists today, all in the name of religion. Even modern Israel is racist, with laws being different for different religious groups.

Science. Modern Western philosophy is acceptance of science as the only knowledge of reality. I.e., mathematical scientific theories, coupled with experiments and observations, along with human experience, are the only source of knowledge.

We must oppose all claims to the contrary, both in our writings, and in our schools. No source of knowledge beyond man's reasoning and observations. No values beyond human life. No life after death.

Christianity is wrong, for their ideas are in conflict with modern Western philosophy. Their ideas are not only wrong, but evil to both individuals, and as a cause for anti-Semitism. Perversion of human nature and clear thinking.

There are very few religious Christian scientists, while there are many Jewish scientists.

Clearly God does not exist within science. Science is, by definition, a collection of mathematical theories combined with physical observations and experiments. The theories are true to the extent that their conclusions agree with observations and experiments. The theories are collections of symbols, definitions and axioms using these symbols, rules of logic and symbol manipulations, and the resulting theorems. For a theory to contain God, it would be necessary to have a symbol represent God, and to define axioms involving God. God cannot be put into a mathematical framework out of which a physical theory will be built. When we speak about science, we cannot speak about God.

Atheism. It is necessary to clarify the concepts we are dealing with, namely atheism and theism. Smith in *"Atheism - The Case Against God"*, by George H. Smith (Nark Publishing. Co., Los Angeles, CA, 1974) defines atheism as "the absence of a belief in God." *Britannica* (Encyclopedia Britannica, 1-666, in section "Atheism," 26-613, in section "Religious and Spiritual Belief" 1985) defines it as "the critique and denial of God." In more precise terms, atheism is defined by the *Britannica*-- as one who rejects belief in God for the following reasons:

"For an anthropomorphic God, it is false or probably false that there is a God. For the God of

Maimonides, such a God is meaningless. For the God portrayed by some modern theologians, the concept of God is such that it merely masks an atheistic substance."

Agnostics are therefore either atheists (if they say that God is meaningless), or theists. The criterion for classifying one as an atheist or a theist is not whether he believes God exists, but whether he claims God is meaningless.

When we say that God is a meaningless idea, we are not saying that the idea of God is meaningless. The human mind has an unlimited potential of creating ideas and ideas, and this is dealt with by science. The God idea has played a major role in history. In this paper, when speaking about God, we refer to God as an ontological being, either imminent or transcendental, not to the God that is merely a product of the human mind.

In today's world there is no need for theism. There is neither a philosophical nor a scientific need for God. Atheism is in full agreement with science.

To quote Hanbury Brown in "*The Wisdom of Science*", Hanbury Brown (Cambridge U. Press, New York, 1986), reviewed by Melba Phillips, *Am. J. Phys.*, **55**, 1154, December, 1987: "By the beginning of the present century it had been established that the physical world could be understood and controlled without invoking God." Phillips paraphrases Brown: "Why then do we need religion? Because most people believe in

God. As an enlightened scientist he deplores the
rise of cults that rest on fixed untenable beliefs
and hold to the literal interpretation of the myths
of Genesis. He rejects the idea of any supernatural
intervention in the physical world. Even the more
enlightened churches are said to be out of step
with the virtues of science - its flexibility,
capacity for change, and the pursuit of truth."

Theism, as a philosophical system, arose out of a
need to explain reality, saying that the world
could not be as perfect and wonderful as it is
unless it was created by God. David Hume and
Immanuel Kant gave powerful critiques of
traditional attempts to prove the existence of God.
The Britannica states that there is considerable
consensus among philosophers that arguments of
this type show that no proof of God's existence is
possible. The world indeed could be perfect and
wonderful without being created by God. From
this it follows that one can understand and accept
reality without God, that is, there is no need for
theism. This is although the human notion of God
has major social and political consequences.

Be proud to defend your ideas, and so do not
claim agnosticism; instead, say you are an atheist.

III. Other religions

Is the Jewish God the same as the God of Islam?
At first, one may think indeed so. How then can
the Jew say that the God of Islam is false if the
Jew believes in the same God? How can the Jew

criticize the religious beliefs of other people if the Jew also believes in the irrational? Most people simply shy away from this problem. One simply does not hear rational discussions about the existence of God. It is considered too sensitive to discuss in public, and if one merely says that God exists, but does not dwell on the topic, he or she will be accepted by most people. We somehow feel that rejecting religion means rejecting morality and living a life devoid of meaning. Furthermore, since Jews throughout history have proclaimed their belief in one God, and have given their lives for His Name, it is very difficult to deny the existence of God. This is the dilemma of modern man. We cannot reject religion, but we know that the idea of God does not make sense.

Russell in *"Why I am Not a Christian"*, by Bertrand Russell (Simon and Schuster, 1957) wrote many powerful arguments against Christianity. However, since the Church is powerful and wealthy, and sponsors considerable university research, one sees in the library many books defending the concept of God, with very few rejecting this concept, giving the mistaken impression that Western thinking is in agreement with Christian thinking. Russell's arguments regarding Christianity are today as valid as when he wrote them.

Smith (*Ibid.*) has also raised very powerful arguments against theism. These arguments, however, apply principally to Christianity. He makes the following points:

1. It is self-contradictory to say that man must renounce reason in order to advance human welfare.

2. Since it is logically impossible to reconcile reason and faith, it follows that belief in God is irrational to the point of absurdity.

3. Due to the irrationality of theism, many religionists simply state that the atheist has psychological problems.

In the above sections we established the lack of a need for theism, and the impossibility of introducing God within science. In this section the intrinsic conflict between Christianity and atheism is discussed. It is important to make this point before discussing Judaism, because Western civilization was founded by Christianity, and many basic Christian ideas are accepted as Western ideas, by people including Jews, even though there is no need for these ideas, and that they run counter to Judaism.

Most religions have a ready answer to the argument that atheism does not contradict religion. Once one confesses belief, the religious leaders are satisfied, as is proven by the Church's acceptance of Galileo's public repudiation of his works. In Judaism, on the other hand, a verbal confession is meaningless if it is insincere, as Maimonides states: "If a person continually says that he believes in God, it is of no value if he does not comprehend this in his mind." *Catholicism wants a formal declaration of belief, while Judaism asks for a true belief.*

We must try then to understand what then the significance of God in Judaism is. What is the meaning of the *Shema*: "Hear O Israel, the Lord our God is One"? It is not an affirmation of conviction to the modern philosopher that atheism is false, for the verse does not state that God is a meaningful idea! The only possible meaning is a statement of our conviction of the unity of the world, and of the existence of one reality. *We are declaring our rejection of multiple realities.*

Today Judaism fights against the occult, against drug-taking trips, against esoteric metaphysical ideas, and against any corporeal (physical) notion of God. The Jewish message to the world is that of unity. We have to deal with the world that we see, for there is no other world. This is a very important message that has to be carried to our society that accepts drugs and alcohol as means to escape reality in order to enter another reality. The Jewish message is that there is no other reality.

Men of God
Yes, the Church leaders are men of God. Since God is a meaningless nonsensical idea, there is no such thing as God. Therefore the church leaders are men of nonsense. The same for the Muslims, who kill for the sake of their nonsense. Be religious if you like the morals and the society, but do not accept nonsense. Do not confuse

religion with reality.

God and Science Don't Mix

A number people have written Letters to the
Editor on the subject of science, replying to
Lawrence Krauss's "God and Science Don't Mix".
These letters indicate sad and dangerous
misunderstandings of science.

Let us begin by discussing mathematics.
Mathematics is a collection of arbitrary
self-consistent statements. For example,
Euclidean and hyperbolic geometries have
statements that contradict each other, but are
internally consistent. The word "truth" is not
applicable to mathematics. We can only discuss
consistency. Furthermore, note that since the
postulates of mathematics are arbitrary, they are
human creations.

When we compare the results of a mathematical
system to the world, using experiments or
observations, we get a scientific theory. The
theory is valid to the extent the experiments agree
with the mathematics. A theory is not a
hypothesis, which is a guess. Although the
mathematical system must be totally consistent,
all experiments are partial. For example,
Newton's theory of gravitation yields results
consistent with observations of planetary motions.
There is a slight discrepancy with the orbit of
Mercury. This is explained by Einstein's theory of
gravitation, which, of course, reduces to Newton's
theory for the orbits of the other planets.

In summary, a scientific explanation of observed phenomena is a mathematical system expanded into a physical theory, by noting the correspondence of various mathematical terms with physical ideas. This is what we mean by rational thinking.

There are two sticky points. *One is that all observational verifications must be partial. There cannot be an absolute truth.*

The other point is that all knowledge is partial. This was proven by K. Gödel, a friend of A. Einstein. Gödel's proof is so difficult to understand that most of us simply do not have a clue about it. What Gödel proved is that for any logical system there will be true statements that cannot be proven from the initial assumptions. This means that one can never have a scientific theory that will explain everything.

Having said this, let us examine the Letters to the Editor. One asked, "On what basis can an atheist assume there should or will be order in the universe?" The answer is that we are not assuming anything. We are simply creating arbitrary statements that must be consistent.

Science may or may not have an explanation of where the world came from. As of today, there is no scientific theory, although there are a number of hypotheses. We said above that science cannot explain everything. "Without an eternal omnipotent being, Mr. Krauss must conclude that the universe, ultimately, came from nothing." Science makes no statement on this topic, and so does not conclude anything.

The question of morals or beauty is not part of science, as there is no mathematical system basing morality. This does not mean that morality does not exist. It merely means that science cannot explain morality. Again, science cannot explain everything.

Prof. Woolley says, "Science came into being and flourished in the West and not within other cultures precisely because of the faith of the curious who believed they were part of a rational universe." Okay, if you wish to discuss the origin of science and scientists. Let us not get lead astray with these thoughts and forget just what science is.

There are important lessons we must learn about science. One is that science may be wrong, such as if we find an inconsistency in the mathematics or a gross contradiction between theory and experiment. The scientist must be able to state that contemporary ideas are wrong. We must learn this lesson today, for too many of us are afraid to say that the President is wrong.

Another lesson is that scientific truth requires both mathematics and experiment; pure thought alone is not science. When the President makes certain policy statements, and we discuss them without comparing them with similar situations in history or other places, we act in a non-scientific manner. It would behoove us not to be quick accepting politician's words. We need to ask ourselves two questions. One is that if we understand the logic of the proposed policy. The other is what can we say about similar places and times where this policy was applied. We are not acting this way with Obama's proposals, and so we are not acting rationally. The faith we have in science is the belief that if we act rationally, trying to understand the reasoning, and comparing with history, we will be better off.

All scientific knowledge is partial.
We need to think about the implications of this important idea, that all scientific knowledge is partial. A medical doctor recommends a certain course of action. Rational thinking demands that we seriously consider doing the opposite, being careful of understanding the risks. If the risks are small enough, we should consider examining the opposite.

In politics, we have something similar. The political leaders exhort us to follow a certain approach, for if not, things would be much worse. We need to spend more money on stimulating the economy, for if not the economy would be worse. Our response must be to demand an alternative approach, namely no stimulus and major tax cuts for the rich, and to see if this helps the economy. When we listen to discussions of national policy, the discussions are focused on efforts to understand government action, not on serious thought to do the very opposite of what is currently done. The attitude is that we must trust our leaders. This is wrong. Since all knowledge is partial, our leaders could be wrong.

People who have overconfidence in their doctors or political leaders do not understand the nature of the scientific revolution that has taken place during the past several centuries.

The situation with Muslims is far worse. They have had no exposure to modern scientific thought. All education is rote learning. *People are compelled by force to follow traditional mannerisms and thought.* The challenge of modern society is to expose Islam to modern science and to understand that all knowledge is partial. We need people to understand that knowledge is acquired by rational thinking, understanding, and acceptance, not by rote and force. We need to be direct and firm in our dealings with Muslims, and not allow them to use emotions and phony word sophistic arguments to fight us. We cannot relax and say that these are simply their beliefs, and we have our beliefs. No! There are not two sides, one side rational thinking, the other emotional authoritative. There is only one side, the side of rational thinking, and we cannot yield to stupidity if we are to survive!

I was talking to a recent college graduate about this. She expressed surprise, as she thought that things are black and white. It is sad that her higher education failed to give her the message of the nature of science. We need to examine how science is presented in our schools, starting with middle school and continuing to college.

9. Science

Although science should be the ultimate in impartial rational thought, the reality is that human emotions prevent important ideas from being expressed.

Black Hole of Light (*Science News*: 3/8/2008, p. 149): A black hole is in a geometrical sense an end to the universe. If we picture the universe using Euclidean geometry, we can imagine going straight out forever. As we approach a black hole, the huge mass changes the geometry so that we also go on forever reaching the surface. We cannot therefore speak about the "inside" of a black hole. The final state of an observer falling down is the singularity at the center of the black hole. A singularity is a division by zero. This means the solution is not valid.

The statement "Black holes are regions where … nothing inside can escape" is false, and contrary to basic concepts in physics.

The only things that have meaning in science are things that can be observed or measured. Gravitation slows time. We all know this, as time on earth is slower than time on a satellite, and this difference is critical for the operation of a GPS, Global Positioning System. As the mass of a star increases, time will slow down on the star's surface so much that it stops if the mass is large enough. It takes forever for an object to reach the surface of a black hole.

RELATIVITY

Albert Einstein
1879-1955

Assumptions of general relativity

Newtonian physics is based upon the principle
that objects move in flat (Euclidean) space, with
forces guiding the motion. Newton's fundamental
equation is $F=ma$. This means the sum of forces
on an object cause the velocity of the object to
change. An object's motion depends upon forces.
In GR, on the other hand, motion is in a curved
4-space and is caused by the curvature. Mass
causes the curvature. These curved lines are
called geodesics. Motion is along these geodesics,
in analogy to force-free motion in a straight line

in flat space.

Let us look at what curvature is. We understand a simple 2-dimensional curved surface, for this is the surface of the earth. An example of a geodesic on this surface is the equator. A more complicated 2-dimensional curved surface is the saddle of a horse. Imagine two fleas moving along the saddle, starting from the same point. Look at one flea. We need a parameter to describe the geodesic the flea is moving. The flea thinks it is moving along a straight line, whereas it really is moving along a curve. We need a second parameter to specify the starting point. To understand the curvature, we have to look at the second flea starting from the same point moving along a different line, and we need a third parameter to describe this line. Finally, we need to compare these two lines, by drawing a line between them, and this is a fourth parameter. Wow, is this complicated! This is why GR is so complicated. This four-parameter object is called the Riemann curvature tensor.

We can simplify this mathematically by summing over two parameters, and get a two-parameter object, called the Ricci tensor. Weinberg in his 1972 book *Gravitation and Cosmology* made certain assumptions about this Ricci tensor, which is discussed below in more detail. He then arrived at the Einstein field equations, EFE, and then said that agreement with observations proves the truth of the assumptions. Wrong. It is possible that simpler assumptions are all that we need for the observations to agree. Hynecek (*PHYSICS*

ESSAYS **23**, 3, 2010) stated a simpler assumption, which is that motion is due to curvature of space. We do not need the "simplification" of the Ricci tensor and its assumptions in order to get equations that agree with observations. Hynecek makes Weinberg's complicated discussion unnecessary.

For a more complete discussion about assumptions and observations, see my recent paper: *Basic assumptions and black holes* (*PHYSICS ESSAYS* **22**, 4 2009).

Since a theory of physics consists of a consistent mathematical framework along with empirical verification, we must not lose sight of the observations verifying the theory. We must not assume the theory is valid if we do not have observations. Black holes are very far away, the nearest one being at the center of our galaxy. Since we cannot observe many details about objects falling into black holes, as they are so far away, we must not assume that we know the physics by assuming present theory will explain it. Maybe we can get agreement with observations by assuming the object at the center of our galaxy is merely a very dense compact object, not a black hole. Unfortunately, this logical fallacy exists in many articles physicists write for the general public.

One reason for such unquestioning support of Einstein's theories may be the very aura of Einstein. I discussed this in a published article, *philica.com*, article number 192. Indeed, the aura of Aristotle meant that for many centuries his wrong idea that velocity is caused by force was the accepted idea until Newton came along.

Correspondence on general relativity
To a physics professor:

I read your interesting articles on teaching special relativity, SR. I have given a lot of thought to the subject. While studying for my doctorate, I saw something that was not right in Panofsky's book on EM. After considerable correspondence with him and others, I published a paper discussing all the wrong ideas people had. What surprised me was that 75 years after this very simple theory was developed, people still were confused, misunderstanding the principles. Now I am thinking about GR. It seems that some of the assumptions are not correct. I see people as confused about this complicated theory as they were about the simple SR. I tried to publish, and a reviewer said an assumption of SR is the speed of light must be constant! It pleased me to read how you demolish this statement!

Here are some questions we must answer:

- How do we teach GR?
- What are the basic assumptions of GR? They need to be stated in clear mathematical form.
- Are these assumptions consistent?

Can we use other assumptions to derive equations

different from the EFE that satisfy all the various observational tests? It is quite possible that the EFE are wrong, but fortuitously give results that agree with observations. This is logically possible, as all observations involve moderately weak fields. All observations about large fields, such as the center of our galaxy, merely indicate a huge compact mass, but there are no observational effects that can clearly be uniquely ascribed to the EFE.

The definition of field at an event (x,t) is the force on a test particle at the event divided by the mass of the particle. Weinberg in his 1972 book stated that a field can act on the field (gravitation is nonlinear). This means that the force on a test mass depends on the force on another test mass somewhere else. This does not make logical sense, as it contradicts the meaning of a test particle.

Another question is Weinberg's second assumption that the trace of the curvature tensor, the Ricci tensor, vanishes in a mass free zone. Again, this does not make clear logical sense. Furthermore, how can we devise a thought experiment to test this? Do you suggest to put a Ricci detector in a cave on the moon, to see if there is any difference. Indeed, what would a Ricci detector be?

Another serious question is the proven singularity at the center of a black hole. A singularity simply means the theory is false there, as division by zero is not permitted. Unfortunately, too many people misunderstand this word! If the theory is false there, the theory is false period. Let us not say that quantum mechanics may come to the rescue. First, no quantum relativity currently exists. Secondly, if there should be developed a valid, consistent quantum gravitation, it will be a different theory from GR, which means the objections stand. We must look at GR without thinking about quantum effects.

Letter to another professor
Sir, you were right saying that the vanishing Ricci in a mass free zone is a conclusion, not the premise in the discussion deriving the EFE. I was confused in that Einstein started with the vanishing Ricci to derive the field equations. In any case, there are troubling points that need clarification. One point you make is that since mass is attracted to the gravitation field, gravity is nonlinear. You make this point without any discussion, such as questioning if is it necessary and how we can experimentally or observationally verify it. Specific examples always help. I always give specific concrete examples to my students. Let us imagine the simplest case, that of two masses orbiting each other. Mass A is attracted to mass B and to the gravitational field between them. How would the motion be described? How would the finite speed of propagation affect the motion? I have never seen any discussion about this point.

The next point you make is the statement that the

tensor T vanishes where there is no mass. I am trying to understand this point. Let us examine electromagnetism. In the empty, charge-free zone between two charged capacitor plates energy exists - recall the displacement vector. However, in the empty, mass-free zone between two masses there is no energy. This does not look right. One needs to explain the difference between electromagnetic theory, EM, and gravitation. We need to clarify why in a charge free zone in EM there is energy, but in a mass-free zone there is no energy so that the stress-energy tensor vanishes.

Physics is stagnating. One reason is the difficulty of publishing ideas which are novel, different from usual accepted ideas. The current assumption physicists have is that the Einstein field equations are necessary to agree with Newtonian gravitation in the limit, and also agree with the various GR tests. It is possible that another set of equations may satisfy these requirements; however, anyone who has ideas about this cannot get published.

In summary, we need to write clear, mathematically precise statements of the assumptions underlying GR. We also need to express ideas how these assumptions can be modified while simultaneously yielding agreement with observations.

Letter to another physicist
Someone quoted you in your textbook "it is perfectly meaningful to talk about someone

falling into a black hole and crossing the event horizon." No, it is meaningless, as it cannot be observed. Remember, science is not religion. A religious person may believe in going to Heaven after death. Science cannot discuss this, as Heaven cannot be observed. The "inside" of a black hole is equally meaningless.

I looked at your *Lecture Notes.* It is not clear exactly what you say the postulates of general relativity are. You try different things and try to show they are reasonable. No good. You must clearly state the postulates of GR. Weinberg did this in his 1972 book. I have one problem with Weinberg. He says a postulate is non-linearly. This is contradicted by observations of satellite orbits. A satellite attracted to the moon and the earth is not attracted to the center of mass of the earth and moon.

GPS
This is a letter to an experimental physicist.

Using the equations of GR increases GPS accuracy from miles to feet. I am surprised why people do not mention this as verification.

It would be nice if we can do experiments to see if photons gravitate. I think the effects are far too small, and will remain so.

Moving charges create magnetic fields that act on other moving charges. I think the same effect is true in GR. However, the effects are too small to observe.

The difficulty of performing experiments with gravity means people can say what they want. People believed in the earth-centric theory of the solar system for generations due to the difficulties of observations. What observations they were able to perform they were able to reconcile with the earth-centric theory by complicated mathematics.

Maxwell's equations, ME, start with Coulomb's law and Lorentz covariance. Suppose we did the same for gravity. Start with Newton's law for the attraction of two masses, and assume Lorentz covariance. We will get ME for gravity, including gravity waves. If we did this, would the results agree with the current verification of the existence of gravity waves?

Light traveling freely in space does not produce a gravitational field, according to John A. Gowan, published on the Internet: http://www.johnagowan.org/lightfield.html. However, light does have momentum and energy, and in this sense has mass. This is an interesting experimental question.

Review in amazon.com
Here is a discussion regarding my comments about black holes. The people involved in this discussion seemed to me to be students, but not very versed in physics.

Mr. P, you said, "But the theory is consistent and

the paradoxes go away as your understanding improves." No. Understanding is not something that just improves. If you understand it better, you must be able to clearly write your new understanding. You must say what the paradox was, and what made it go away. I say there is no paradox. Just that the solution of the equations from the falling observer's viewpoint crossing the Event Horizon, EV, is not a valid solution. No paradox. Just not a valid solution.

Your statement, "If someone tells you that one observer's reference frame is 'meaningful'". No. Meaningful means meaningful to all observers, as all observers can measure the events.

"Another interesting observation is that if you take any curved surface and zoom in closely enough, it looks flat…" This is true as long as space is continuous, whereas the EV is a discontinuity.

"So if you were falling into a black hole (and you were the size of a particle), in principle there would be no way to tell that you have crossed the event horizon..." Since your falling into the Black Hole, cannot be observed, it is not part of reality. Again, this solution is false.

"This is like saying that we cannot apply our laws of physics to galaxies at distances comparable to the Hubble Ultra Deep Field because we cannot directly observe the fact that they work there…" We can in principle observe these galaxies.

"Aranoff claims that trajectories which cross the event horizon of a black hole should be discarded as unphysical…" Yes. We just ignore these trajectories, and look at those that do not. E.g., the vibrating string. We discard as unphysical all solutions of the wave equation that violate the boundary conditions.

Mr. P, you said you are attending a working group on relativity. Very good. However, you must remember that all that they can teach you are various mathematical ideas and tricks, along with the conclusions of the difficult mathematics. You have to keep an open mind regarding the basic ideas. Since all science is based upon partial empirical verification, we know that the basic assumptions may change. New theories will arise; however, these theories must agree with existing theories to the extent that the existing theories agree with observations. Einstein's GR is very different from Newtonian gravitation; however, it must agree with Newton regarding the moon's orbit and tides. This is your challenge as a physics student. Understand the mathematics, assumptions, conclusions, empirical evidence, and opportunities to challenge existing assumptions without contradicting current evidence. Good luck! Do not allow yourself to be swayed by personality or popularity. Try to understand, and think how you would explain it to others. If you cannot explain it to a student, you do not understand it. Find some students to whom you can explain what you learned at the seminar.

....

Mr. P, your comments reminds me after getting my PhD, I noticed something confusing in Panofsky's book on E&M. He was a world famous physicist, head of Stanford Linear Accelerator Center. After a lot of correspondence, I wrote some papers in peer reviewed journals on Special Relativity. It amazed me that so many experts in relativity failed to understand simple ideas of this simple theory. The same is true today with GR. You can read this in my 1972 paper, *Equilibrium in Special Relativity,* on my website, http://www.analysis-knowledge.com/msgTeaching.htm.

Another interesting paper is *"The Galileo effect and the general relativity theory"* by Jaroslav Hynecek, PHYSICS ESSAYS **22**, 4, 2009.

Bottom line: A physical theory has two parts: a math part and empirical verification. The math must be consistent. The theory is valid to the extent of the verification. Newtonian theory gives an orbit to Mercury that does not fully agree with observation. Einstein's theory does give the correct orbit. On the other hand, with extreme gravitational fields, we do not have clear evidence. Hynecek and Bekenstein have shown that alternate theories to Einstein agree with current observations. I disagree with your statement that all university professors agree with you.

Okay, you insist on Einstein's solution from the viewpoint of the falling observer crossing the event horizon. You insist that this is a valid concept in physics in spite of the fact that no observer outside the BH can observe this. I say you are wrong in your understanding of science.

Here is an interesting example. Cool helium gas and liquefy it. You can imagine the liquid consists of molecules bouncing around. Continue cooling it below the lambda temperature, 2.17 K. It becomes a Bose-Einstein liquid. We cannot imagine it consisting of molecules bouncing around. Since we cannot empirically determine the locations of the molecules, except to say somewhere in the container, we cannot speak about molecules. Instead we talk about rotons and phonons. Again, no molecules, just rotons. Same with the observer falling down the BH. He never gets there.

....
From: John B

I intuitively grasp your statement "Approaching a BH is geometrically similar to moving eternally outwards to the 'end' of the universe."

I also imagine that when A looks back at me, on Earth, my signal is getting weaker as he accelerates away from me. (I wonder if, from his point of view, what he is "leaving behind" looks like a black hole to him.)

B....

My response:
Read *Gravitation* by Misner et. al., discussion about the signal of an object approaching a BH. It becomes redshifted and disappears. The object falling is Traveler *A*. The observer is one who is not falling, Traveler *B*. When you talk about time on watches, do not forget time dilation due to gravitational fields. *A*'s watches are slower, just as watches on earth are slower than watches on a satellite, a critical effect for GPS.

When *A* crosses the EV, he loses all contact with the universe. To me this is identical to religious nonsense that dead go to heaven, are aware of heaven, while the living are not. Since this idea of heaven is sheer nonsense, the crossing of the EV is also nonsense - not a valid solution of the equations of GR.

Plasma physics
A plasma is an electrically conducting fluid. The material at the surface of the sun is a plasma. The vastness of space inside a galaxy is a plasma. Although the material is extremely rare, the vast scale makes it equivalent to a plasma.

Science News published an article entitled, "*Cosmic Evidence of a Smooth Beginning*" (SN: 1/20/1990, p. 36). The article did not contain any mention of plasma physics.

There are magnetic fields in the space of a galaxy.

There are gravitational fields, due to the stars. The stars move, and so have kinetic energy. The equipartition of energy theorem states that the energy densities in the galaxy of magnetic fields, gravitational fields and kinetic energy are comparable in magnitude. Therefore, the large energies associated with magnetic fields (plasmas) must have some effect in the structure of galaxies.

I can understand why computer simulations of galaxies ignore plasma effects, due to the difficulties of incorporating such effects in the programs. But I cannot understand why theoretical discussions simply ignore plasmas.

The most pleasing theory of cosmology from an intellectual standpoint is the steady-state theory of Fred Hoyle. It is based upon the strong symmetry principle - namely, that there is symmetry in the large in the universe in space-time. There can be no fundamental difference in the universe here or anywhere else, or at any time. This theory lost favor due to difficulties with observations. However, recent observations and modern theoretical developments may yet rescue it.

There are other theories of physics that negate the Big Bang.

The interesting question is: How do certain theories become so accepted that other theories of equal validity cannot even be heard? How many papers dealing with such other theories are rejected by referees? Is the Big Bang in favor due to religious feelings?

The three-body problem

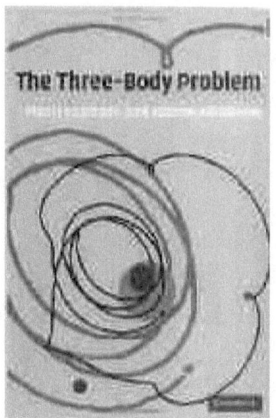

Newtonian gravitation is a subject children learn in school. The planets orbit the sun in almost perfect circles. The mathematical equations are easy enough for a high school student to deal with and solve.

What about the three-body problem, such as a satellite attracted to the earth and the moon? The equations are so hard that they cannot be solved. We can get approximate solutions using computers. The computer solutions tell us surprising things, such as there are paths in space from one point to another that require very little energy. If we travel space in rocket ships, and are willing to spend a lot extra time traveling, we can make our journeys with very little fuel. This reminds us of sailing ships centuries ago who crossed oceans without fuel, relying only on wind and currents.

Since the Newtonian three-body problem is so interesting, one wonders what is the situation using Einstein's theory of gravitation for the three-body problem. My feeling is that we need to investigate this, so that we can compare observations with theory and use this as a means of testing Einstein's theory.

Here are some letters I wrote on the topic:

You said in 1997 that GPS provides a rich source of examples for the applications of the concepts of relativity. What is the situation today? Distances and times change due to general relativity. In addition, there is a perturbation of the motion of the satellite due to gravitational attraction to the gravitational field (gravitation self-attraction, or nonlinear effects). My feeling is that present day calculations achieve very high accuracy of GPS, to within feet, completely ignoring nonlinear effects, and this can be used to say that evidence points to the nonexistence of nonlinear effect.

*****

Jay Mireles James
You are involved with the 3-body problem. This is very interesting, for numerical calculations are required and can be verified by observations of satellite orbits. According to usual interpretations of GR, a mass is attracted not only to another mass but also to the gravitational field of the masses. A satellite is attracted to the sun and to the earth. As it moves along, there are regions

where the gravitational field is stronger, such as when the earth and sun line up. Are these effects taken into account? If not, then the observed agreement of the calculations with the observations would suggest the non-existence of the assumed gravitational self-force. Hynecek derived equations that satisfy the usual tests for general relativity, but have no gravitational self-force. Satellite orbit calculations and observations would be a very important test for general relativity.

The world is like a fish bowl

Prof. Hawking said the world is like a fish bowl. This is a metaphor. Just as the fish is aware only of the bowl, and not of the reality of the room, we people may be aware only of the universe we see, and unaware of possible universes outside of our universe. Other physicists have said similar things.

This is a serious mistake, grossly misunderstanding the nature of science. There are two types of situations. One situation consists of observations we cannot explain. We know, based upon Gödel's work, that there will always exist observations that no current theory can explain. The other situation consists of observations that current theories explain.

For the first type, unexplained observations, we must be careful not to act like primitive pagans, who explained things saying the gods did it. We must not say there is another reality beyond science that can explain it. We must avoid acting like the ancient Egyptians who believed in the existence of another universe where people went after death. Instead, we must accept the fact that we do not have an explanation, and spend efforts to finding explanations. The research may have to fight political pressures from people who think they know the answers and are not interested in research.

The second type consists of valid theories. If a theory states that something cannot be observed, then it does not exist within the framework of the theory. An example is the "inside" of a black hole within the theory of General Relativity, for the theory states that this cannot be observed. Another example is the position of molecules of superfluid helium. The theory tells us that we can only say the molecules are in the container. As liquid helium cools below the lambda point, the meaning of the positions disappear.

When Hawking and others speak about other universes, they refer to the first type, unexplained observations, for currently there is no valid theory of cosmology that unifies gravitation and quantum mechanics. They are reverting to primitive paganism, trying to say things that sound scientific but really are not. It is sad that leading scientists do not properly understand the philosophy of science, and consequently mislead the public.

Time

There is, unfortunately, a great deal of false and misleading ideas put out by scientists today. The reason is excessive attention to the process and calculations of science, ignoring fundamental principles. The best example is discussions about the nature of a black hole. The statement, often heard, that a black hole is a region of space with such a large gravitational field that nothing can escape, is simply false. The correct statement is that a black hole is a region of space where the spacetime geometry is so extremely distorted that it takes forever for anything to reach it. It is nonsense to speak about the inside, for there is no inside in this extreme geometry.

Recently *Science News* had an article about time. Again, we must not forget fundamental principles of physics. Length is defined as that which is measured with a ruler. Time is defined as that which is measured by a clock. The future does not exist, as it did not yet happen. The past does not exist, as one cannot go into the past, for if so, it would not be the past. The only reality is the present, which includes records, such as pictures and memories, of past events. Time does not "flow", for it does not make sense to measure this flow, that is, there is no way to measure this flow. The reason for the direction of time is clear – we have records of past events, not of future events.

A few physicists have written books and articles on this topic, but it seems that these correct ideas have gotten lost with all the other ideas on this topic.

I wrote a proper discussion of this in a paper: " *Time Does Not Exist and the Incompleteness of Knowledge*," *philica.com*, article number 188, Aranoff, S. (2010).

Stem-cell research

Opponents of the stem-cell research program say, "The research is unproven." *All research is unproven*. This is the nature of research, as all evidence is based upon statistics. Human beings seek out the unknown and try to understand the universe. In addition, research brings enormous benefits to mankind. We must do all we can to encourage research. We must increase funding, even in times of critical shortages of resources. We must support both private and public research, and try our best to encourage people to enter scientific research as careers.

Opponents of stem-cell research say that the issue is moral. No, the issue is religious, not moral. Microscopic cells are not people. If you wish to believe that these cells are people, that is fine, but please do not impose your beliefs on me. The world has enough troubles with many Moslems using force and murder to advance their beliefs to others who reject them. America is based upon separation of religion from government. The government must not get involved with the religious issue of whether stem cells are people or not.

American jobs going overseas may be due to our

weakening commitment to basic scientific research. Our diminishing faith that scientific research is necessary for progress is causing the current economic stagnation. Our country will continue to decline because we are not sufficiently engaged in free thought and scientific research.

Animosity toward science
Why so much animosity toward science? The answer is poor education, and not knowing what science is.

This is what science is. Science is understanding the world based upon fundamental principles. The principles can be changed, but must be consistent along with partial empirical verification. E.g., we look at stars at night. They are not simple points of light in the sky, but distant suns. The principles of gravitation correctly predict ocean tides. Who cares? Answer: I care. I want to know things. Don't you? Teachers should encourage questioning. When they insist on simply paying attention, as President Obama said, they are not educating. We need to know how to think rationally. Our schools do not do enough. University professors should spend some time teaching high school classes.

Some incorrectly think that the purpose of science is to benefit humanity. Scientists should choose projects that can best benefit humanity. Wrong! The purpose of science is to understand the world we live in. Why? Because! We do not want to live

in ignorance, limiting ourselves to perform
scientific research only for areas that can benefit
humanity.

Scientific research is not a waste of money. Do
not make fun of scientists for not doing
something constructive.

When I was a 7-year old, I told my friends that the
stars were actually distant suns. They laughed at
me in disbelief. The attitude is that since it makes
no difference to people, why even talk about stars
really being suns. Wrong!

What is with our education system in the U.S. that
such unfortunate ignorance is prevalent?

Global warming
Prof. J. R. Kuhn said, "A period of solar
overheating allowed Vikings to cultivate grain on
Greenland." Wow! We thought that global
warming was caused solely by human production
of energy! Maybe our leaders, including
prospective leaders, should rethink signing the
Kyoto protocols, which aim to reduce production
of carbon dioxide. If the current warming is due
to the sun, there is no point in wasting money on
Kyoto.

Index